June 1993

CORE ENGLISH

That's Entertainment!

Ronald Caie, Hellen Matthews,
Anne Mitchell and Anne Rigg

SERIES EDITOR:
Colin Lamont

HEINEMANN EDUCATIONAL BOOKS

Heinemann Educational Books Ltd
22 Bedford Square, London WC1B 3HH

LONDON EDINBURGH MELBOURNE AUCKLAND
SINGAPORE KUALA LUMPUR NEW DELHI KINGSTON
IBADAN NAIROBI JOHANNESBURG PORTSMOUTH (NH)

First published 1986
Reprinted 1987 (twice)

That's entertainment! – (Core English)
  1. English literature – 20th century
  I. Caie, Ronald II. Series
  820.8'00914   PR1148

  ISBN 0–435–10584–1

Typeset by Fakenham Phototypesetting Ltd,
Fakenham, Norfolk
Printed and bound in Great Britain by
Richard Clay Ltd, Bungay, Suffolk

CONTENTS

Acknowledgements

The authors and publishers wish to thank the following for permission to reproduce copyright material. It has not been possible to contact all copyright holders, and the publishers would be glad to hear from any unacknowledged copyright holders.

R E C Burrell for 'The Roman Amphitheatre' from *The Romans and Their World*; Jonathan Cape and the Executors of the Estate of C Day Lewis for 'Circus Lion' from *The Gate*; Jonathan Cape for 'Goldilocks and the Three Bears' from *Revolting Rhymes* by Roald Dahl and Quentin Blake and 'The Pleasure Drome' from *Under Plum Lake* by David Line (Lionel Davidson); David Higham Associates Limited for 'Henry' from *Man and Beast* by Phyllis Bottome, 'Colonel Fazackerley' by Charles Causley from *Figgie Hobbin* and 'Holiday Memory' from *Quite Early One Morning* by Dylan Thomas; Laurence Pollinger Ltd and the Estate of Mrs Frieda Lawrence Ravagli for 'Elephants in the Circus' by D H Lawrence; Aberdeen College of Education for 'Clown Song' from *Fifth Estate* by Val McDermid; Michael Joseph Ltd for 'All the Fun of the Fair' from *Late, Late in the Evening* by Gladys Mitchell and 'The Ants at the Olympics' from *Animal Alphabet* by Richard Digance; 'Flight of the Roller Coaster' is reprinted from *Collected Poems of Raymond Souster* by permission of Oberon Press; 'The Word Market' is from *The Phantom Tollbooth* text © Norton Juster 1961, published by Collins; Penguin Books Ltd for 'William's Version' and 'Nothing to be Afraid Of' from *Nothing to be Afraid Of* by Jan Mark (Kestrel Books, 1980), copyright © Jan Mark, 1977, 1980; Stephen Mulrine for 'A Gude Buke'; 'Footy Poem' and 'A Good Poem' from *In the Glassroom* © 1976 by Roger McGough and 'Pantomime Poem' from *After the Merrymaking* © 1971 by Roger McGough are reprinted by permission of A D Peters & Co Ltd; Michael Gibson and Macmillan, London and Basingstoke for 'The Ice-Cart' from *Collected Poems 1905–1925* by Wilfrid Gibson; Macmillan, London and Basingstoke for the extract from *The Machine Gunners* by Robert Westall and 'The Seaside' by James Gibson from *Solo and Chorus*; Methuen Children's Books and Mervyn Peake for 'My Uncle Paul of Pimlico' from *Rhymes Without Reason*; Gareth Owen for 'Ping Pong' and 'The Fight'; George Allen & Unwin and J R R Tolkien for 'Bilbo's Party' from *The Fellowship of the Ring*; John Murray (Publishers) Ltd for John

Betjeman's poem 'False Security' from *Collected Poems*; Molly Weir for the extracts from *Shoes Were For Sunday* and *Best Foot Forward*; The Salamander Press, Edinburgh for 'Tinsel' from *It's Colours They Are Fine* by Alan Spence; 'There Are No Lights on our Christmas Tree' composed by Cyril Tawney © 1968, reproduced by permission of Gwyneth Music Ltd/Dick James Music Limited, London; London Management for the extract from *Kidnapped at Christmas* by Willis Hall; Vernon Scannell for 'Autobiographical Note'; Captain Beaky Limited (Reg'd trademark Captain Beaky T.M.) for 'Daddy-Long-Legs' by Jeremy Lloyd from *The Captain Beaky Book Volume I*, 1976 Chappell Music Ltd; Harvey Unna & Stephen Durbridge Ltd for the extract from *Unman, Wittering and Zigo* by Giles Cooper.

Illustrations:

Mark Urgent: pages 20, 98, 120; Colin Robinson: pages 22–23, 45, 57; Al Burton: pages 24, 26, 44, 50, 87, 112–113; Dave Farris: pages 31, 69, 78–79, 110–111; Murray Aikman: pages 40, 62, 102; Nicky Marsh: pages 48–49, 52; Anthony Kerins: pages 46–47, 81; Mander & Mitchenson Theatre Collection: page 3; Mansell Collection: page 7; Rex Features Ltd: pages 8, 9, 12, 16; Mary Evans Picture Library: page 94; Syndication International: page 95; The Photo Source: page 114.

1

Circuses

Circuses have a long and interesting history. We might think of them now as being part of television entertainment, but the circus is one of the oldest live forms of entertainment.

The word *circus* originally meant a circle or a ring and comes from the Roman circuses, huge rings which were built with stone seats for the spectators. One of the biggest was the Circus Maximus where men raced chariots pulled by horses.

There were also open air places called amphitheatres with raised seats round an arena. Gladiators fought with each other there and sometimes with wild animals kept in cages under the raised seats. Wild animals from Africa were taken to Rome to amuse the Romans, and bears, lions, elephants, tigers and bulls were put together so that they would fight and provide entertainment for the spectators. We are very aware nowadays of how animals are treated and would consider these shows cruel and dangerous, but huge crowds went to watch them.

The Romans built arenas in some towns in England, including Chester and Dorchester, and in France and Spain. Some of the Spanish arenas are used today to stage bullfights.

Travelling Circuses

These are modern circuses which we recognise, where the circus arrives in town, the big top is put up, and the show remains for perhaps a week before moving on.

These evolved from small zoos which began travelling from town to town, often when the town fair was being held. After the buying and selling had been done people would watch the animals, and such acts as rope walkers and sword swallowers. Later the acts were put together and the separate entertainers joined up with performing animals to make up one big show.

Astley's Circus

Philip Astley, who lived in the eighteenth century, is sometimes said to be the founder of today's circuses. After riding horses in the army he started a show in a field in London where he performed trick riding stunts. He went on to be very successful, opening 19 circuses all over Europe and presenting massive spectacles like water pantomimes. He had many rivals who also opened their own circuses.

Circus nowadays is a completely international art. You only need to look at a circus programme to see that there are acts from countries all over the world working together. The famous Russian state circuses are among the most impressive. There is even a private language spoken by circus people everywhere.

Clowns

Most young children would think immediately of clowns if asked about circuses generally, and yet the clowns are often used as 'fill-in' between acts. Because much of their work is done in mime, language is unimportant and clowns have a truly international appeal. Their dress is perhaps the first thing we think of; traditionally the clown wears a baggy costume often with pom-poms and is made up in a characteristic way. Normally his face is white with large painted lips and emphasised eyes; often he has a false nose. Clowns use make up to emphasise expressions. They can make themselves look permanently happy, sad, surprised or anxious.

Although we refer to them all as clowns there are really two different types. A clown is the white-faced man in the spangled costume: the man with the false nose and baggy suit is correctly called an Auguste. These two often work in pairs to make people laugh, sometimes with the traditional water and custard pies.

Two of the most famous clowns were Joseph (Joey) Grimaldi in the nineteenth century who set the tradition of the white-faced clown, and Coco the Clown, one of the most popular characters in the British circus.

Anne Mitchell

2
The Roman Amphitheatre

If you wanted to see men die, the amphitheatre was the place for you, not the circus. The word *amphitheatre* means 'a theatre on both sides'. The original Greek theatre was a half-circle of terraced seats where plays were performed, and for a while, such plays were mildly popular in Rome. But the plays sank into low pantomime where absolutely anything was allowed to happen on the stage. It was not uncommon for a condemned criminal to be executed as part of the play.

It is an unfortunate streak in the Roman character that they really enjoyed this sort of coarse brutality, and to create the proper setting for it they built amphitheatres, the most famous (or perhaps 'infamous') of which was the Flavian amphitheatre better known as the Colosseum. It could seat 45,000 people.

In the Colosseum, during the reign of the Caesars, thousands of men and animals were butchered 'to make a Roman holiday'. The custom seems to have been borrowed from the Etruscans, who, tiring of just executing their prisoners of war, armed them and made them kill each other.

Like chariot racing, the 'games', as they were called, probably had a religious origin. The first gladiatorial combats in Rome, of which there is any record, took place in 264 BC. The first to have official blessing were arranged by the two Consuls for the year 105 BC. Thereafter they were staged to mark a celebration or a victory.

From being seasonal and occasional, they gradually grew longer and more frequent. At the beginning of the imperial period, more than seventy days a year were given up to these disgusting exhibitions, and by its end, almost half the year was a holiday for the 'games'. These were, of course, only the regular fixtures – emperors could and did finance extra fights whenever they felt like it. It was quite common for them to last for weeks: there are records of more than one such 'extra' going on continuously for one hundred days!

It has been said that the Caesars provided the people with *panem et circenses* (bread and circuses) to keep them quiet and to prevent them from protesting too strongly at the miserable lives they were forced to lead. It is true that men were ready and willing to flood the arena with all the fanatical excitement they had once given to politics. Once the republic had come to an end there were no politics for the people, so they flocked into the Colosseum and took their seats. Often the emperor himself could be seen in his ringside box, surrounded by his family and his favourites.

The proceedings usually started with a procession of gladiators who halted in front of the royal box and chanted, *'Ave! imperator. Morituri te salutant!'* (Greetings, O Emperor. We who are about to die salute thee!) These men were recruited from the ranks of the slaves, ex-prisoners of war, condemned criminals and the like. Sometimes they were free-born men who for one reason or another had made a mess of their lives, or who fancied themselves as fighters. After all, a successful gladiator could become almost as rich and famous as a chariot driver.

The first exercises were designed to warm up the crowd. Men with wooden staves and whips fought each other. This was not normally fatal. Neither was the next item which consisted of men fencing with wooden swords. The crowd fidgeted and waited impatiently for the real business to begin. To relieve the boredom of such moments, some emperors had the crowd bombarded with small tokens, any one of which might win its lucky holder a fortune. On the other hand, when he turned up at the palace to collect his prize, he might find that he was the proud owner of a rotten cabbage!

At last the waiting was rewarded by the sight of the officials walking slowly out to the centre of the sandy arena. By now the sun would be getting high in the sky, and sailors from the imperial fleet would be ordered to unroll canvas awnings over the tiers of seats. When the 'referees' reached the middle, the crowd fell silent. The first weapons to be used were of razor-sharp metal, and the crowd had to be shown that there was no trickery. At the same time, lots were drawn for the death fights. This was also done in public.

Gladiators were of several different kinds: some were completely armed, some only partly. One sort of fighter had a fish-spear, or trident, and a large net; others would perform on horseback or from a chariot. Most of the helmets they wore had a metal grille which acted as a face mask.

The normal pattern in the early days was for men to be matched according to their armour and their skill. Some emperors, however, found it amusing to pit a net thrower against a swordsman, or a cavalryman against a charioteer. There were other unequal combats – two strong men against five weak ones, and the inevitable man-against-animal fights.

5

In the 'standard' match, however, two men faced each other, only too well aware that the probable outcome for one of them was death. You can imagine with what care they stalked one another, how fiercely they attacked and with what brutality they stabbed when an opponent was at their mercy.

If he could still move, a defeated gladiator would raise one hand, imploring mercy from the emperor. The latter would stand up and make a great show of consulting the crowd. If a man had fought well, people would signal with their thumbs and the loser would be spared. His relief would later turn to despair when the thought struck him that he still had it to do again on a future occasion. But if he had put on a display the mob didn't like, they would say so in no uncertain manner and he would be killed.

Criminals were often executed in the arena as a sort of interlude. Their number often included Christians whose only crime was a refusal to worship a statue of the emperor. The heroic way they met their fate made quite a few converts for Christ, and by the fourth century AD, his followers were able to oppose the games openly. Steadily they won support for their point of view, and in 313, the emperor Constantine put an end to three centuries of Christian persecution. From that time onward a number of laws were passed cutting down the length and size of the games. Training schools for gladiators were closed and servants of the government were forbidden to have anything to do with them. But it was not until the beginning of the fifth century that the emperor Honorius, who loathed these exhibitions, had a reasonable excuse to ban them.

It was provided by a Christian monk, named Telemachus, who was lynched when he tried to separate two gladiators. Animal baiting, however, appears to have continued long after the Roman empire had fallen to the barbarians. As late as the end of the seventh century, men were still fighting lions, tigers and panthers in the arenas of Rome.

During its long and blood soaked history, the Colosseum alone must have witnessed hundreds of thousands of senseless deaths, and this was but one of the many amphitheatres scattered the length and breadth of the empire.

History has probably nothing to compare with this demoralizing spectacle of blood-crazed spectators, howling and jeering at the death agonies of animals and of fellow human beings. Once 5,000 animals were slaughtered in a single day, and it is said that the beast-catchers who worked in the jungles and deserts of the world for the circuses were responsible for the extinction of whole species of animals in particular areas.

Upon another occasion, 5,000 pairs of gladiators fought to the death to make an afternoon's entertainment for the callous crowds of the eternal city. In sheer numbers of victims, only Hitler's Germany can offer any parallel.

Today the Colosseum stands silently brooding on its gory past: hordes of tourists click their cameras and then move on to the next attraction. Only a cross bears mute testimony to the martyrs who perished there.

R. E. C. Burrell

3

Elephants in the Circus

Elephants in the circus
have aeons of weariness round their eyes.
Yet they sit up
and show vast bellies to the children.

D. H. Lawrence

Circus Lion

Lumbering haunches, pussfoot tread, a pride of
Lions under the arcs
Walk in, leap up, sit pedestalled there and glum
As a row of Dickensian clerks.

Their eyes are slag. Only a muscle flickering,
A bored theatrical roar
Witness now to the furnaces that drove them
Exultant along the spoor.

In preyward, elastic leap they are sent through paper
Hoops at another's will
And a whip's crack: afterwards, in their cages,
They tear the provided kill.

Caught young, can this public animal ever dream of
Stars, distances and thunders?
Does he twitch in sleep for ticks, dried water-holes,
Rogue elephants, or hunters?

Sawdust, not burning desert, is the ground
Of his to-fro, to-fro pacing,
Barred with the zebra shadows that imply
Sun's free wheel, man's coercing.

See this abdicated beast, once king
Of them all, nibble his claws:
Not anger enough left – no, nor despair –
To break his teeth on the bars.

C. Day Lewis

4

Henry

For four hours every morning, and for twenty minutes before a large audience at night, Fletcher was locked up with murder.

It glared at him from twelve pairs of amber eyes; it clawed the air close to him, it spat naked hate at him, and watched to catch him for one moment off his guard.

Fletcher had only his will and his eyes to keep death at bay.

The lion-tamer in the next cage was better off than Fletcher. He stripped himself half-naked every night, covered himself with ribbons, and thought so much of himself that he hardly noticed his lions. Besides, his lions had all been born in captivity, were slightly doped; and were only lions.

Fletcher's tigers weren't doped and they hated man.

Fletcher had taught tigers since he was a child; his father had started him on baby tigers, who were charming. They hurt you as much as they could. What was death to you was play to them; but as they couldn't kill him, all the baby tigers did was to harden Fletcher and teach him to move about quickly. He knew when a tiger was going to move, and moved quicker so as to be somewhere else.

After a few months the baby tigers could only be taught by fear, fear of a whiplash, fear of a pocket pistol which stung them with blank cartridges; and above all the mysterious fear of the human eye. When he was only ten years old, Fletcher had learned never to show a tiger that he was afraid of him. 'If you ain't afraid of a tiger, you're a fool,' his father told him, 'but if you show a tiger you're afraid of him, you won't even be a fool long!'

The first thing Fletcher taught his tigers, one by one in their cages, was to catch his eye, then he stared them down. He had to show them that his power was stronger than theirs.

The next stage was to get them used to noise and light. Tigers dislike noise and light, and they wanted to take it out on Fletcher when he exposed them to it.

When it came to the actual trick teaching, Fletcher relied on his voice and a long stinging whip. The lion-tamer roared at his lions; Fletcher's voice was not loud; but it was as noticeable as a warning bell, it checked his tigers like the crack of a pistol.

For four hours every morning, Fletcher frightened his tigers into doing tricks. He rewarded them as well; after they had been frightened enough to sit on tubs, he threw them bits of raw meat.

Fletcher took them out one by one at first and then rehearsed them gradually together. It was during the single lessons that he discovered Henry.

Henry had been bought, rather older than the other tigers, from a drunken sailor.

For some time afterwards, Henry snarled at all the keepers, showed his teeth and clawed the air close to Fletcher's head exactly like the eleven other tigers, only with more vim. He was a very fine young tiger, exceptionally powerful and large. Every day, Fletcher sat longer and longer, closer and closer to Henry's cage, watching.

The first day he went inside, there seemed no good reason, either to Henry or to himself, why he should live to get out. The second day something curious happened. While he was attempting to outstare Henry, and Henry was stalking him to get between him and the cage door, a flash of something came into Henry's eyes. He stopped stalking and sat down. Fletcher held him firmly with his eyes; the great painted head sank down and the amber eyes blurred and closed under Fletcher's gaze. A loud noise filled the cage, a contented, pleasant noise. Henry was purring!

He threw down his whip, Henry never moved; he approached Henry. Henry permitted the approach. Fletcher took his life in his hand and touched Henry. Henry snarled mildly, but his great claws remained closed; his eyes expressed nothing but a gentle warning, they simply said: 'You know I don't like being touched, be careful, I might have to claw you!' Fletcher gave a brief nod; he knew he could do something with Henry.

Hour after hour every day he taught Henry, but he taught him without a pistol or a whip. It was unnecessary to use anything beyond his voice and his eyes.

He used to sit for hours at the back of his cage waiting for Fletcher. When he heard the sound of Fletcher's step, he moved forward to the front of his cage and prowled restlessly to and fro till Fletcher unlocked the door and entered. Then Henry would crouch back a little. As soon as Fletcher spoke, he came forward proudly.

Henry liked doing his tricks alone with Fletcher. He jumped on and off his tub following the mere wave of Fletcher's hand. He soon went further, jumped on a high stool and leapt through a large white paper disc held up by Fletcher.

He let Fletcher sit on his back. He stood perfectly still, his hair rising a little, his teeth bared, a half growl in his throat.

It was with Henry and Henry alone that Fletcher dared his nightly stunt, dropped the whip and stick at his feet and let Henry do his tricks as he did them in his cage alone, with nothing beyond Fletcher's eyes and voice to control him. The other eleven tigers sat on their tubs glaring and snarling. He had the chance they had always wanted, and he didn't take it – what kind of tiger was he?

But Henry ignored the other tigers. Fletcher stood in front of him with a stick between his hands and told Henry to jump from his tub over his head. What Fletcher said was: 'Come on, old thing! Jump! Come on! I'll duck in time. You won't hurt me! It's my stunt! Stretch your old paws together and jump!' And Henry jumped. He hated the dazzling lights, loathed the senseless sounds which followed his leap, and he was secretly terrified that he would land on Fletcher. But it was very satisfactory when after his rush through the air he found he hadn't touched Fletcher, but had landed on another tub carefully prepared for him.

The circus manager spoke to Fletcher warningly about his foolish trust of Henry.

'Mark my words, Fletcher,' he said, 'the tiger doesn't live that wouldn't do you in if it could. You give Henry too many chances – one day he'll take one of them!'

But Fletcher only laughed. He knew Henry. Fletcher boasted of Henry to the lion-tamer.

Macormack, the lion-tamer, had a very good stunt lion, and he was very jealous of Henry. He could not make his lion go out backwards before him from the arena cage into the passage as

Henry had learned to do for Fletcher: and when he had tried, Ajax had flung him against the bars of the cage.

Macormack said, 'Why don't yer put yer 'ead in 'is mouf and be done with it? That ud be talking, that would!'

'I wouldn't mind doing it,' said Fletcher after a brief pause, 'once I get him used to the idea. 'Is jaw ain't so big as a lion's, still I could get the top of me 'ead in.'

The lion-tamer swaggered off jeering, and Fletcher thought out how best to teach Henry this new trick.

But from the first Henry didn't approve of it. He showed quite plainly that he didn't want his head touched. He didn't like his mouth held open, and wouldn't have anything put between his teeth without crunching. Fletcher wasted several loaves of bread over the effort. Henry roared long and loudly at him and clawed the air. He decided not to go on with the trick.

'It ain't fair to my tiger!' he said to himself regretfully; and he soothed Henry with raw meat.

But when the hour for the performance came, Fletcher forgot his promise. He was jealous at Macormack's stunt lion for getting more than his share of the applause.

Henry jumped through his white disc – so did the stunt lion. He took his leap over Fletcher's head – the stunt lion did something flashy with a drum, not half as dangerous, and the blind and ignorant audience ignored Henry and preferred the drum.

'I don't care!' said Fletcher to himself. 'Henry's got to take my head in his mouth whether he likes it or not – that'll startle 'em!'

He got rid of all the other tigers. Henry was used to that, he liked it; now he would do his own final stunt – walk out backwards into the passage which led to the cages, and Fletcher would hurry out through the arena and back to Henry's cage, give him a light extra supper, and tell him what a fine tiger he was.

But Fletcher called him into the middle of the stage instead and made him take that terrible position he had taught him for the new trick. His eyes said: 'You'll do this once for me, old man, won't you?'

Henry's eyes said: 'Don't ask it! I'm tired! I'm hungry! I want to get out!'

But Fletcher wouldn't read Henry's eyes. He tried to force his head sideways into the terrible open jaws, and Henry's teeth closed on Fletcher's neck.

Phyllis Bottome
(Adapted)

13

5
Fall Guy

When the army taught Michael Costello a thing or two about using explosives in warfare, little did they know what they were starting. To a man like Michael, with his Irish circus background, it was only a matter of time before he incorporated a few sticks of dynamite into his escapology act. Now, it's not unusual for him to climb into a coffin twice a day and blow himself up.

That of course is not the only talent of stuntman international Blondini. In his time he's slept on beds of nails, pulled cars along with his teeth, jumped off buildings, fallen off bridges, escaped from straightjackets ... and he used to be a human cannonball until someone stole his cannon.

Now, he says, 'stunting isn't what it was. Gimmicks have taken over in film-making and everyone's playing for safety.' He reckons the public aren't fooled for a minute and he is constantly on the lookout for new ways to defy death that will leave his audiences gasping.

'The public love to see danger. That's what they pay for,' he says. 'They wouldn't like to see you injured but they love to see you come as close as possible–it's human nature.'

Michael learned these lessons early as he was brought up among the thrills and spills of circus life. His father did a strongman act, his mother was a highwire artiste. As a youngster Michael was a bareback rider, then went on to fire-eating and sword-swallowing.

When he came out of the Army he began doing escapology in the theatre. But he injured his shoulder through the contortions necessary to wriggle out of ropes and chains, and so started experimenting with explosives. Now he performs stunts like The Coffin of Death and Cage of Fire at open-air shows all over the world.

His base is a rather untidy Victorian house on the outskirts of Manchester where he lives with his wife Sally. She assists in his act and studies Egyptology at the University of Manchester in her spare time. When their travels of the summer season grind to a halt, Michael spends the winter months planning new feats for the forthcoming year. Currently he's working out how to dive from a great height into 50 cm of water.

It seems superfluous to ask why he does it. It's the only thing he knows and it's clear he enjoys the glamour and excitement. The fact that he regularly suffers serious burns and injuries is something he has come to accept with the same resignation as the rest of us accept income tax.

'Some people think I'm mad to do these stunts. And thank God they do because that's why they pay to see me,' he says. He's had cracked ribs and punctured lungs, he's had teeth knocked out and his worst injuries came when he was suspended from a 20 m pole in a straitjacket and the rope broke. That laid him up for 11 months.

His record for hospital treatment was four visits in three days when his coffin explosives stunt at Nottinghamshire gala hit a run of bad luck. 'Every time the bang went, out came the ambulance and away I went,' he recalls. 'Everything went wrong. Eventually the doctor said, "If you're determined to commit suicide, we don't want you down here." And I didn't blame him.'

But, he says, 'these incidents don't happen all the time. I go a whole season and nothing happens. Then something goes wrong and bang, bang, bang. Accidents seem to come in threes.'

Michael is very superstitious and he never travels on the 13th. He always says a quiet prayer before his act.

He swears there is no trickery in his performance. 'It's knowing how to lay the dynamite, that's the skill of it. And controlling your breathing so you slow the heart-rate right down.'

His Cage of Fire stunt, when he lies in an ignited wooden box soaked with petrol, brought him close to suffocation recently and a colleague was badly burned rescuing him. But there is only one stunt he really regrets. When he was 'buried alive' for 78 days it shattered his nerves.

Although he has been close to death many times, his fear of dying is, surprisingly, perhaps stronger than in most of us.

Only one thing holds more terror for Blondini and that's if he gets a mysterious pain in the chest during the day. 'I'm petrified of having a heart attack,' he said. 'I'd much rather die doing a stunt because if you get injured, you have time to weigh things up and make your peace with your Maker. But a heart attack can snuff you out just like that.'

Judi Goodwin

Clown Song

Laugh at the clown, I'll do a somersault for you
I'll make you smile, laugh, or cry, just what you want me to
Behind my mask, you don't see the tears
I've been crying now for all of sixteen years
But I can't show my sorrow for I'm the clown.

Look at me leap, I'm a flying troubadour,
But don't follow me behind the caravan door.
I wouldn't shatter the dreams you hold,
For though I'm young, my eyes are very old
I would not hurt you, for I'm the clown.

Watch me tumbling, I'm a living laughter box
I take my mask off for a few, they can withstand the shock,
For inside me I'm a twisted soul,
My eyes are prophetic within their holes
They don't show behind my mask, for I'm the clown.

Laugh at my fun, I want you to smile at me
Be happy outside, your smiling faces I want to see
I wouldn't want your faces sad like mine,
But go home, take off your masks, perhaps you'll find
The joke is not on me, for you're the clowns.

Val McDermid

All the Fun of the Fair

The fair had its roots in the dim and distant Middle Ages, but the only remaining vestiges of its original function, which was annual trading in goods brought by merchants from miles around and even from foreign parts, were the small booths and stalls on the outskirts of the space occupied by roundabouts and swings and all the other exciting and noisy pleasures on which most of the people (and especially the children) had come to spend their money.

Kenneth and I were in a fever all day. We had hoped to set off immediately after breakfast and spend the whole day at the fair, but Uncle Arthur thought otherwise. After tea was the time to go, he said, so Aunt Kirstie made us rest after the mid-day dinner and when, at last, we were ready to set off, she made us wear our overcoats and told Uncle Arthur on no account to keep us out late.

It was a long way to the bus stop and a long way from the bus terminus to the fair, or so it seemed to me at the age of ten. However, we could hear the raucous music as soon as we turned into Broad Street and I know our steps quickened at the sound of it.

St Swithin's Fair had nothing to do with St Swithin's legendary rain-making. It was so called because it was held in St Swithin's market-place, a large open square behind the covered market where we were taken for an occasional treat to eat lardy-cakes and look at the puppies, kittens, cage-birds, Angora rabbits, Belgian hares and Flemish giants in the pet-shop. I can still remember the mingled odours and scents of the covered market – the sour smells of small animals, the heavenly smells of baking, flowers and fruit, the sweaty smell of people and the moist, earthy smell of freshly-watered ferns and plants in pots.

The fair was entirely different from the covered market. It was far more exciting. At any rate, it wildly excited Kenneth and me. We had expected much, but I am bound to say that St Swithin's Fair was no disappointment. Looking back now, after all these years, I realise that few things to which young children (after all, I was only ten years old and Kenneth eight) look forward, do turn out to be disappointing. Youthful imagination coupled with a desperate desire for wish-fulfilment sees to that, and therefore St

Swithin's Fair stands out in my mind as one of the high spots in a moderately happy life. We did not need to seek for any kind of compensation. We thoroughly enjoyed ourselves.

For one thing, Uncle Arthur was to our minds an ideal companion, an easy-going, simple-minded, very indulgent sort of man. He was not native to the village, but came of Cockney ancestors. His mother was a virago who was accustomed literally to throw her husband and sons into the street when they came home drunk, and she had bestowed her thews and sinews and her generous, single-minded outlook, but not her flaming temper, upon Uncle Arthur. He had boxed in the East End for small purses, so was technically a professional, but he was a kindly man who lacked the killer instinct which brings a boxer fame and the big money.

At the fair he soon gave a taste of his muscular quality. He banged with a mallet on a sort of anvil and a weight shot up and rang a bell. He was given a cigar for that. Then he smashed a coconut and was given a whole one in exchange. We were thrilled and delighted, so much so that 'a penn'orth on the mat,' which he urged us to try, made me forget my fears of this sort of feat. I cascaded round the bends with some enjoyment and returned slightly dizzy but undoubtedly triumphant to Kenneth and Uncle Arthur after I and my mat had been fielded by a sweating man in a dirty singlet who stood at the foot of the tower.

After all these years, some of my impressions of the fair are rather blurred, like the reflections of brilliant lights on wet pavements while the rain is still pouring down. I remember that, although it was not yet dark when we arrived, the naked naphtha flares which lit up the scene were already hissing and windblown. I remember the jostling, shoving, good-humoured crowds, the gaily-painted swing-boats, and the raucous, heady, intoxicating music blaring from the roundabouts.

I remember that I nearly (but not quite) ringed a most desirable box of chocolates at the hoop-la stall and that Kenneth tried his luck with an airgun but failed to hit one of the ping-pong balls which were dancing up and down on jets of water, and I remember arguing with him as to whether or not you got a longer ride on the roundabout by taking one of the outside horses rather than one nearer the centre where the machinery and the music were.

'It stands to reason,' he said. 'It's a case of concentric circles. The outside one has the longest perimeter.'

'But it travels slower,' I said, 'so the actual length of the ride is the same.'

We tried a swing-boat with Uncle Arthur at one end and the two of us at the other. I did not like this very much because, as the boat swung higher, it seemed quite possible that at a certain point we could go clean over the top and loop the loop, so I was relieved when our time was up and the man in charge grounded us with a long wooden plank which jarred the boat uncomfortably and alarmingly but soon brought us to a standstill.

Uncle Arthur bought us bullseyes, brandy snaps and lardy-cakes and we drank so-called lemonade. Later on we had sausage rolls and ice-cream. (Ice-cream was a rare treat in those days and we seldom bought it for ourselves because it disappeared so quickly.) Soon after this, a clock on St Swithin's church struck ten and Uncle Arthur decided that it was time to think about going home.

Gladys Mitchell

8
A Street Acrobat

When I first came out I wasn't above two years old, and my father used to dance me on his hands. I can just recollect being danced in his hands, but I can't remember much about it, only he used to throw me a somersault with his hand.

When father first trained me, it hurt my back awfully. He used to take my legs and stretch them, and work them round in their sockets, and put them straight by my side. That is what they call being 'cricked', and it's in general done before you eat anything in the morning.

Oh, yes, I can remember being cricked, and it hurt terrible. He put my chest to his chest, and then pulled my legs up to my head, and knocked 'em against my head and cheeks about a dozen times. It seems like as if your body was broken in two, and all your muscles being pulled out like india rubber.

I worked for my father till I was twelve years of age, then I was sold for two years to a man of the name of Tagg, another showman, who took me to France. He had to pay my father £5 a year, and keep me respectable.

I ran away from Tagg in Paris, and I went with the 'Frères de Bouchett', rope dancers, and I had to clown to the rope. They had a large booth of their own, and it was mostly at fairs.

From then I came to England, and began pitching in the street. I didn't much like it, after being a regular performer, and looked upon it as a drop. I travelled right down by myself to Glasgow fair.

I kept company with Wombwell's show – only working for myself. You see, they used to stop in the towns, and draw plenty of people, and then I'd begin pitching to the crowd. I had a suit of tights, and a pair of thwacks with a few spangles on, and as soon as people came round me I began to work.

Recorded by Henry Mayhew,
19th century historian

9
The Freaks

In the early autumn of every year the Chattahoochee Exposition came to town. For a whole October week the fair went on down at the fair grounds. There was the Ferris Wheel, the Flying Jinney, the Palace of Mirrors – and there, too, was the House of the Freaks. The House of the Freaks was a long pavilion which was lined on the inside with a row of booths. It cost a quarter to go into the general tent, and you could look at each Freak in his booth. Then there were special private exhibitions farther back in the tent which cost a dime apiece. Frankie had seen all of the members of the Freak House last October:

> The Giant
> The Fat Lady
> The Midget
> The Wild Nigger
> The Pin Head
> The Alligator Boy
> The Half-Man Half-Woman.

The Giant was more than eight feet high, with huge loose hands and a hang-jaw face. The Fat Lady sat in a chair, and the fat on her was like loose-powdered dough which she kept slapping and working with her hands – next was the squeezed Midget who minced around in little trick evening clothes. The Wild

Nigger came from a savage island. He squatted in his booth among the dusty bones and palm leaves and he ate raw living rats. The fair gave a free admission to his show to all who brought rats of the right size, and so children carried them down in strong sacks and shoe boxes. The Wild Nigger knocked the rat's head over his squatted knee and ripped off the fur and crunched and gobbled and flashed his greedy Wild Nigger eyes. Some said that he was not a genuine Wild Nigger, but a crazy coloured man from Selma. Anyway, Frankie did not like to watch him very long. She pushed through the crowd to the Pin-Head booth, where John Henry had stood all afternoon. The little Pin Head skipped and giggled and sassed around, with a shrunken head no larger than an orange, which was shaved except for one lock tied with a pink bow at the top. The last booth was always very crowded, for it was the booth of the Half-Man Half-Woman, a morphidite and a miracle of science. This Freak was divided completely in half – the left side was a man and the right side a woman. The costume on the left was a leopard skin and on the right side a brassiere and a spangled skirt. Half the face was dark-bearded and the other half bright glazed with paint. Both eyes were strange. Frankie had wandered around the tent and looked at every booth. She was afraid of all the Freaks, for it seemed to her that they had looked at her in a secret way and tried to connect their eyes with hers, as though to say: we know you. She was afraid of their long Freak eyes. And all the year she had remembered them, until this day.

Carson McCullers

Flight of the Roller-Coaster

Once more around should do it, the man confided. . . .

and sure enough, when the roller-coaster reached the peak
of the giant curve above me, screech of its wheels
almost drowned out by the shriller cries of the riders,

instead of the dip and plunge with its landslide of screams,
it rose in the air like a movieland magic carpet, some wonderful
    bird,
and without fuss or fanfare swooped slowly across the
    amusement-park,
over Spook's Castle, ice-cream booths, shooting-gallery. And
    losing no height

made the last yards above the beach, where the cucumber-
    cool
brakeman in the last seat saluted
a lady about to change from her bathing-suit.

Then, as many witnesses reported, headed leisurely out over
    the water,
disappearing all too soon behind a low-flying flight of clouds.

Raymond Souster

The Word Market

Before long they saw in the distance the towers and flags of Dictionopolis sparkling in the sunshine, and in a few moments they reached the great wall and stood at the gateway to the city.

'A-H-H-H-R-R-E-M-M,' roared the sentry, clearing his throat and snapping smartly to attention. 'This is Dictionopolis, a happy kingdom, advantageously located in the Foothills of Confusion and caressed by gentle breezes from the Sea of Knowledge. To-day, by royal proclamation, is market day. Have you come to buy or sell?'

'I beg your pardon?' said Milo.

'Buy or sell, buy or sell,' repeated the sentry impatiently. 'Which is it? You must have come here for some reason.'

'Well, I—' Milo began.

'Come now, if you don't have a reason, you must at least have an explanation or certainly an excuse,' interrupted the sentry.

Milo shook his head.

'Very serious, very serious,' the sentry said, shaking his head also. 'You can't get in without a reason.' He thought for a moment and then continued. 'Wait a minute; maybe I have an old one you can use.'

He took a battered suitcase from the sentry box and began to rummage busily through it, mumbling to himself, 'No . . . no . . . no . . . this won't do . . . no . . . h-m-m-m . . . ah, this is fine,' he cried triumphantly, holding up a small medallion on a chain. He dusted it off, and engraved on one side were the words 'WHY NOT?'

'That's a good reason for almost anything – a bit used perhaps, but still quite serviceable.' And with that he placed it around Milo's neck, pushed back the heavy iron gate, bowed low, and motioned them into the city.

'I wonder what the market will be like,' thought Milo as they drove through the gate; but before there was time for an answer they had driven into an immense square crowded with long lines of stalls heaped with merchandise and decorated in gaily-coloured bunting. Overhead a large banner proclaimed:

WELCOME TO THE WORD MARKET

And, from across the square, five very tall, thin gentlemen

regally dressed in silks and satins, plumed hats, and buckled shoes rushed up to the car, stopped short, mopped five brows, caught five breaths, unrolled five parchments, and began talking in turn.

'Greetings!'

'Salutations!'

'Welcome!'

'Good afternoon!'

'Hello!'

Milo nodded his head, and they went on, reading from their scrolls.

'By order of Azaz the Unabridged—'

'King of Dictionopolis—'

'Monarch of letters—'

'Emperor of phrases, sentences, and miscellaneous figures of speech—'

'We offer you the hospitality of our kingdom,'

'Country,'

'Nation,'

'State,'

'Commonwealth,'

'Realm,'

'Empire,'

'Palatinate,'

'Principality.'

'Do all those words mean the same thing?' gasped Milo.

'Of course.'

'Certainly.'

'Precisely.'

'Exactly.'

'Yes,' they replied in order.

'Well, then,' said Milo, not understanding why each one said the same thing in a slightly different way, 'wouldn't it be simpler to use just one? It would certainly make more sense.'

'Nonsense.'

'Ridiculous.'

'Fantastic.'

'Absurd.'

'Bosh,' they chorused again, and continued.

'We're not interested in making sense; it's not our job,' scolded the first.

'Besides,' explained the second, 'one word is as good as another – so why not use them all?'

'Then you don't have to choose which one is right,' advised the third.

'Besides,' sighed the fourth, 'if one is right, then ten are ten times as right.'

'Obviously you don't know who we are,' sneered the fifth. And they presented themselves one by one as:

'The Duke of Definition.'

'The Minister of Meaning.'

'The Earl of Essence.'

'The Count of Connotation.'

'The Under-secretary of Understanding.'

Milo acknowledged the introduction and, as Tock growled softly, the minister explained.

'We are the king's advisers, or, in more formal terms, his cabinet.'

'Cabinet,' recited the duke: '1. a small private room or closet, case with drawers, etc., for keeping valuables or displaying curiosities; 2. council room for chief ministers of state; 3. a body of official advisers to the chief executive of a nation.'

'You see,' continued the minister, bowing thankfully to the duke, 'Dictionopolis is the place where all the words in the world come from. They're grown right here in our orchards.'

'I didn't know that words grew on trees,' said Milo timidly.

'Where did you think they grew?' shouted the earl irritably. A small crowd began to gather to see the little boy who didn't know that letters grew on trees.

'I didn't know they grew at all,' admitted Milo even more timidly. Several people shook their heads sadly.

'Well, money doesn't grow on trees, does it?' demanded the count.

'I've heard not,' said Milo.

'Then something must. Why not words?' exclaimed the under-secretary triumphantly. The crowd cheered his display of logic and continued about its business.

'To continue,' continued the minister impatiently. 'Once a week by Royal Proclamation the word market is held here in the great square and people come from everywhere to buy the words they need or trade in the words they haven't used.'

'Our job,' said the count, 'is to see that all the words sold are proper ones, for it wouldn't do to sell someone a word that has no meaning or didn't exist at all. For instance, if you bought a word like *ghlbtsk*, where would you use it?'

'It would be difficult,' thought Milo – but there were so many words that were difficult, and he knew hardly any of them.

'But we never choose which ones to use,' explained the earl as they walked towards the market stalls, 'for as long as they mean what they mean to mean we don't care if they make sense or nonsense.'

'Innocence or magnificence,' added the count.

'Reticence or common sense,' said the under-secretary.

'That seems simple enough,' said Milo, trying to be polite.

'Easy as falling off a log,' cried the earl, falling off a log with a loud thump.

'Must you be so clumsy?' shouted the duke.

'All I said was—' began the earl, rubbing his head.

'We heard you,' said the minister angrily, 'and you'll have to find an expression that's less dangerous.'

The earl dusted himself, as the others snickered audibly.

'You see,' cautioned the count, 'you must pick your words very carefully and be sure to say just what you intend to say. And now we must leave to make preparations for the Royal Banquet.'

'You'll be there, of course,' said the minister.

But before Milo had a chance to say anything, they were rushing off across the square as fast as they had come.

'Enjoy yourself in the market,' shouted back the under-secretary.

'Market,' recited the duke: 'an open space or covered building in which—'

And that was the last Milo heard as they disappeared into the crowd.

'I never knew words could be so confusing,' Milo said to Tock as he bent down to scratch the dog's ear.

'Only when you use a lot to say a little,' answered Tock.

Milo thought this was quite the wisest thing he'd heard all day. 'Come,' he shouted, 'let's see the market. It looks very exciting.'

12

William's Version

William and Granny were left to entertain each other for an hour while William's mother went to the clinic.

'Sing to me,' said William.

'Granny's too old to sing,' said Granny.

'I'll sing to you, then,' said William. William only knew one song. He had forgotten the words and the tune, but he sang it several times, anyway.

'Shall we do something else now?' said Granny.

'Tell me a story,' said William. 'Tell me about the wolf.'

'Red Riding Hood?'

'No, not *that* wolf, the other wolf.'

'Peter and the wolf?' said Granny.

'Mummy's going to have a baby,' said William.

'I know,' said Granny.

William looked suspicious.

'How do you know?'

'Well . . . she told me. And it shows, doesn't it?'

'The lady down the road had a baby. It looks like a pig,' said William. He counted on his fingers. 'Three babies look like three pigs.'

'Ah,' said Granny. 'Once upon a time there were three little pigs. Their names were – '

'They didn't have names,' said William.

'Yes they did. The first pig was called – '

'Pigs don't have names.'

'Some do. These pigs had names.'

'No they didn't.' William slid off Granny's lap and went to open the corner cupboard by the fireplace. Old magazines cascaded out as old magazines do when they have been flung into a cupboard and the door slammed shut. He rooted among them until he found a little book covered with brown paper, climbed into the cupboard, opened the book, closed it and climbed out again. 'They didn't have names,' he said.

'I didn't know you could read,' said Granny, properly impressed.

'C-A-T, wheelbarrow,' said William.

'Is that the book Mummy reads to you out of?'

'It's my book,' said William.

'But it's the one Mummy reads?'

'If she says please,' says William.

'Well, that's Mummy's story, then. My pigs have names.'

'They're the wrong pigs.' William was not open to negotiation. 'I don't want them in this story.'

'Can't we have different pigs this time?'

'No. They won't know what to do.'

'Once upon a time,' said Granny, 'there were three little pigs who lived with their mother.'

'Their mother was dead,' said William.

'Oh, I'm sure she wasn't,' said Granny.

'She was dead. You make bacon out of dead pigs. She got eaten for breakfast and they threw the rind out for the birds.'

'So the three little pigs had to find homes for themselves.'

'No,' William consulted his book. 'They had to build little houses.'

'I'm just coming to that.'

'You said they had to *find* homes. They didn't *find* them.'

'The first little pig walked along for a bit until he met a man with a load of hay.'

'It was a lady.'

'A lady with a load of hay?'

'NO! It was a lady-pig. You said *he.*'

'I thought all the pigs were little boy-pigs,' said Granny.

'It says lady-pig here,' said William. 'It says the lady-pig went for a walk and met a man with a load of hay.'

'So the lady-pig,' said Granny, 'said to the man, "May I have some of that hay to build a house?" and the man said, "Yes." Is that right?'

'Yes,' said William. 'You know that baby?'

'What baby?'

'The one Mummy's going to have. Will that baby have shoes on when it comes out?'

'I don't think so,' said Granny.

'It will have cold feet,' said William.

'Oh no,' said Granny. 'Mummy will wrap it up in a soft shawl, all snug.'

'I don't *mind* if it has cold feet,' William explained. 'Go on about the lady-pig.'

'So the little lady-pig took the hay and built a little house. Soon the wolf came along and the wolf said – '

'You didn't tell where the wolf lived.'

'I don't know where the wolf lived.'

'15 Tennyson Avenue, next to the bomb-site,' said William.

31

'I bet it doesn't say that in the book,' said Granny, with spirit.

'Yes it does.'

'Let me see, then.'

William folded himself up with his back to Granny, and pushed the book up under his pullover.

'*I* don't think it says that in the book,' said Granny.

'It's in ever so small words,' said William.

'So the wolf said, "Little pig, little pig, let me come in," and the little pig answered, "No". So the wolf said, "Then I'll huff and I'll puff and I'll blow your house down," and he huffed and he puffed and he blew the house down, and the little pig ran away.'

'He ate the little pig,' said William.

'No, no,' said Granny. 'The little pig ran away.'

'He ate the little pig. He ate her in a sandwich.'

'All right, he ate the little pig in a sandwich. So the second little pig – '

'You didn't tell me about the tricycle.'

'What about the tricycle?'

'The wolf got on his tricycle and went to the bread shop to buy some bread. To make the sandwich,' William explained, patiently.

'Oh well, the wolf got on his tricycle and went to the bread shop to buy some bread. And he went to the grocer's to buy some butter.' This innovation did not go down well.

'He already had some butter in the cupboard,' said William.

'So then the second little pig went for a walk and met a man with a load of wood, and the little pig said to the man, "May I have some of that wood to build a house?" and the man said, "Yes."'

'He didn't say please.'

'"Please may I have some of that wood to build a house?"'

'It was sticks.'

'Sticks *are* wood.'

William took out his book and turned the pages. 'That's right,' he said.

'Why don't you tell the story?' said Granny.

'I can't remember it,' said William.

'You could read it out of your book.'

'I've lost it,' said William, clutching his pullover.

'Look, do you know who this is?' He pulled a green angora scarf from under the sofa.

'No, who is it?' asked Granny, glad of the diversion.

'This is Doctor Snake.' He made the scarf wriggle across the carpet.

'Why is he a doctor?'

'Because he is all furry,' said William. He wrapped the doctor round his neck and sat sucking the loose end. 'Go on about the wolf.'

'So the little pig built a house of sticks and along came the wolf – on his tricycle?'

'He came by bus. He didn't have any money for a ticket so he ate up the conductor.'

'That wasn't very nice of him,' said Granny.

'No,' said William. 'It wasn't *very* nice.'

'And the wolf said, "Little pig, little pig, let me come in," and the little pig said, "No," and the wolf said, "Then I'll huff and I'll puff and I'll blow your house down," so he huffed and he puffed and he blew the house down. And then what did he do?' Granny asked, cautiously.

William was silent.

'Did he eat the second little pig?'

'Yes.'

'How did he eat this little pig?' asked Granny, prepared for more pig sandwiches or possibly pig on toast.

'With his mouth,' said William.

'Now the third little pig went for a walk and met a man with a load of bricks. And the little pig said, "*Please* may I have some of those bricks to build a house?" and the man said, "Yes." So the little pig took the bricks and built a house.'

'He built it on the bomb-site.'

'Next door to the wolf?' said Granny. 'That was very silly of him.'

'There wasn't anywhere else,' said William. 'All the roads were full up.'

'The wolf didn't have to come by bus or tricycle this time, then, did he?' said Granny, grown cunning.

'Yes.' William took out the book and peered in, secretively. 'He was playing in the cemetery. He had to get another bus.'

'And did he eat the conductor this time?'

'No. A nice man gave him some money, so he bought a ticket.'

'I'm glad to hear it,' said Granny.

'He ate the nice man,' said William.

'So the wolf got off the bus and went up to the little pig's house, and he said, "Little pig, little pig, let me come in," and the little pig said, "No," and then the wolf said, "I'll huff and I'll puff and I'll blow your house down," and he huffed and he puffed and he huffed and he puffed but he couldn't blow the house down because it was made of bricks.'

'He couldn't blow it down,' said William, 'because it was stuck to the ground.'

'Well, anyway, the wolf got very cross then, and he climbed on the roof and shouted down the chimney, "I'm coming to get you!" but the little pig just laughed and put a big saucepan of water on the fire.'

'He put it on the gas stove.'

'He put it on the *fire*,' said Granny, speaking very rapidly, 'and the wolf fell down the chimney and into the pan of water and was boiled and the little pig ate him for supper.'

William threw himself full length on the carpet and screamed.

'He didn't! He didn't! *He didn't!* He didn't eat the wolf.'

Granny picked him up, all stiff and kicking, and sat him on her lap.

'Did I get it wrong again, love? Don't cry. Tell me what really happened.'

William wept, and wiped his nose on Doctor Snake.

'The little pig put the saucepan on the gas stove and the wolf got down the chimney and put the little pig in the saucepan and boiled him. He had him for tea, with chips,' said William.

'Oh,' said Granny. 'I've got it all wrong, haven't I? Can I see the book, then I shall know, next time.'

William took the book from under his pullover. Granny opened it and read, *First Aid for Beginners: a Practical Handbook*.

'I see,' said Granny. 'I don't think I can read this. I left my glasses at home. You tell Gran how it ends.'

William turned to the last page which showed a prostrate man with his leg in a splint; *compound fracture of the femur*.

'Then the wolf washed up and got on his tricycle and went to see his Granny, and his Granny opened the door and said, "Hello, William."'

'I thought it was the wolf.'

'It was. It was the wolf. His name was William Wolf,' said William.

'What a nice story,' said Granny. 'You tell it much better than I do.'

'I can see up your nose,' said William. 'It's all whiskery.'

Jan Mark

Goldilocks and the Three Bears

This famous wicked little tale
Should never have been put on sale.
It is a mystery to me
Why loving parents cannot see
That this is actually a book
About a brazen little crook.
Had I the chance I wouldn't fail
To clap young Goldilocks in jail.
Now just imagine how *you'd* feel
If you had cooked a lovely meal,
Delicious porridge, steaming hot,
Fresh coffee in the coffee-pot,
With maybe toast and marmalade,
The table beautifully laid,
One place for you and one for dad,
Another for your little lad.
Then dad cries, 'Golly-gosh! Gee-whizz!
'Oh cripes! How hot this porridge is!
'Let's take a walk along the street
'Until it's cold enough to eat.'
He adds, 'An early morning stroll
'Is good for people on the whole
'It makes your appetite improve
'It also helps your bowels to move.'
No proper wife would dare to question
Such a sensible suggestion,
Above all not at breakfast-time
When men are seldom at their prime.
No sooner are you down the road
Than Goldilocks, that little toad
That nosey thieving little louse,
Comes sneaking in your empty house.
She looks around. She quickly notes
Three bowls brimful of porridge oats.
And while still standing on her feet,
She grabs a spoon and starts to eat.
I say again, how *would* you feel

If you had made this lovely meal
And some delinquent little tot
Broke in and gobbled up the lot?
But wait! That's not the worst of it!
Now comes the most distressing bit.
You are of course a houseproud wife,
And all your happy married life
You have collected lovely things
Like gilded cherubs wearing wings,
And furniture by Chippendale
Bought at some famous auction sale.
But your most special valued treasure,
The piece that gives you endless pleasure,
Is one small children's dining-chair,
Elizabethan, very rare.
It is in fact your joy and pride,
Passed down to you on grandma's side.
But Goldilocks, like many freaks,
Does not appreciate antiques.
She doesn't care, she doesn't mind,
And now she plonks her fat behind
Upon this dainty precious chair,
And crunch! It busts beyond repair.
A nice girl would at once exclaim,
'Oh dear! Oh heavens! What a shame!'
Not Goldie. She begins to swear.
She bellows, 'What a lousy chair!'
And uses *one* disgusting word
That luckily you've never heard.
(I dare not write it, even hint it.
Nobody would ever print it.)
You'd think by now this little skunk
Would have the sense to do a bunk.
But no. I very much regret
She hasn't nearly finished yet.
Deciding she would like a rest,
She says, 'Let's see which bed is best.'
Upstairs she goes and tries all three.
(Here comes the next catastrophe.)
Most educated people choose
To rid themselves of socks and shoes
Before they clamber into bed.
But Goldie didn't give a shred.
Her filthy shoes were thick with grime,

And mud and mush and slush and slime.
Worse still, upon the heel of one
Was something that a dog had done.
I say once more, what *would* you think
If all this horrid dirt and stink
Was smeared upon your eiderdown
By this revolting little clown?
(The famous story has no clues
To show the girl removed her shoes.)
Oh, what a tale of crime on crime!
Let's check it for a second time.

Crime One, the prosecution's case:
She breaks and enters someone's place.

Crime Two, the prosecutor notes:
She steals a bowl of porridge oats.

Crime Three: She breaks a precious chair
Belonging to the Baby Bear.

Crime Four: She smears each spotless sheet
With filthy messes from her feet.

A judge would say without a blink,
'Ten years hard labour in the clink!'
But in the book, as you will see,
The little beast gets off scot-free,
While tiny children near and far
Shout: 'Goody-good! Hooray! Hurrah!'
'Poor darling Goldilocks!' they say,
'Thank goodness that she got away!'
Myself, I think I'd rather send
Young Goldie to a sticky end.
'Oh daddy!' cried the Baby Bear,
'My porridge gone! It isn't fair!'
'Then go upstairs,' the Big Bear said,
'Your porridge is upon the bed.
'But as it's inside mademoiselle,
'You'll have to eat *her* up as well.'

Roald Dahl

14
The Lady or the Tiger?

In very olden times, there lived a king who, though he seemed polite and polished, was nevertheless capable of enforcing some very barbaric laws. He was an absolute ruler and, although for the most part, he ruled wisely, when anyone did him wrong or broke any of his strict laws, he could act with sudden cruelty. He liked everything to be clear and well-ordered and was intolerant to all those who opposed him.

One of his chief ideas was the construction of a huge amphitheatre where he entertained his thousands of subjects with shows of a more or less barbaric nature. It was an enormous building with encircling galleries, mysterious vaults and unseen passages. Its chief purpose was not simply to entertain the crowds of the common people by various outrageous events but to provide a dramatic test for any of his subjects unlucky enough to be accused of a serious crime.

When a subject was accused of a crime of sufficient importance to interest the king, it was announced that on an appointed day the fate of the accused person would be decided in the king's arena.

When all the people had assembled in the galleries, and the king, surrounded by his court, sat high up on his throne, he gave a signal, a door beneath him opened, and the accused subject stepped into the amphitheatre. Directly opposite him, on the other side of the enclosed space, were two doors, exactly alike and side by side. It was the duty of the person on trial, to walk directly to these doors and open one of them. He could open either door he pleased. If he opened one, there came out of it a hungry tiger, the fiercest and most cruel that could be found, which immediately sprang upon him, and tore him to pieces, as punishment for his guilt. The moment that the case of the criminal was thus decided, doleful iron bells were clanged, great wails went up from hired mourners and the vast audience with bowed heads wended slowly homewards greatly mourning that one so young and handsome, or so old and respected, should have deserved such a terrible end.

But if the accused person opened the other door, there came out a lady of about his own age, the most beautiful that could be selected from the king's subjects. To this lady he was immediately married as a reward for his innocence. It did not matter that he might already have a wife and family or that he might be in love with someone else. The king would allow nothing to interfere with his great scheme for punishing the guilty and rewarding the innocent. Another door opened beneath the king and a priest, followed by a choir and a band playing on golden horns stepped into the arena accompanied by a troupe of dancing girls. They advanced to where the pair stood side by side and the wedding was promptly performed. Then the brass bells rang out merrily, the people shouted glad hurrahs, and the innocent man preceded by children strewing flowers on his path, led his bride to his home.

This was the king's barbaric method of administering justice. Its perfect fairness is obvious. The criminal could not know from which door would come the lady: he opened either door as he pleased, without having the slightest idea whether in the next instant, he was to be devoured or married. On some occasions the tiger came out of one door, and on some out of the other. The accused person was instantly punished if he found himself guilty; and, if innocent, he was rewarded on the spot, whether he liked it or not. There was no escape from the judgments of the king's arena.

The practice was a very popular one. When the people gathered together on one of the great trial days, they never knew whether they were to witness a bloody slaughter or a hilarious wedding. This uncertainty lent an interest to the occasion. Thus the masses were entertained and pleased and the thinking part of the community could bring no charge of unfairness against this plan; for did not the accused person have the whole matter in his own hands?

The king had a daughter as beautiful as he was barbaric. As is usual in such cases, she was the apple of his eye and was loved by him above all others. Among his courtiers was a young man like one of those conventional heroes of romance who love royal princesses. This royal princess was well satisfied with her lover, for he was handsome and brave and she loved him with a feeling that had enough barbarism in it to make it exceedingly warm and strong. This love affair moved on happily for many months, until one day the king happened to discover its existence. He did not hesitate nor waver in regard to his duty. The youth was immediately cast into prison, and a day appointed for his trial in the king's arena. This, of course, was an especially important occasion; and his majesty, as well as all the people, was greatly interested in the workings and development of the trial. Never

before had such a case occurred; never before had a subject dared to love the daughter of a king. In after-years such things became commonplace enough; but then they were novel and startling.

The tiger-cages of the kingdom were searched for the most savage and relentless beasts, from which the fiercest monster might be selected for the arena; and the ranks of the most beautiful young girls throughout the land were surveyed by competent judges in order that the young man might have a fitting bride in case he avoided the fate of the tiger. Of course everybody knew that the deed with which the accused was charged had been done. He had loved the princess, and neither he, she, nor any one else thought of denying the fact; but the king would not think of allowing any fact of this kind to interfere with the workings of the system. No matter how the affair turned out, the youth would be disposed of; and the king would take great pleasure in watching the course of events.

The appointed day arrived. From far and near the people gathered, and thronged the great galleries of the arena; and crowds unable to gain admittance, massed themselves against its outside walls. The king and his court were in their places opposite the twin doors, so terrible in their similarity.

All was ready. The signal was given. A door beneath the royal party opened and the lover of the princess walked into the arena. Tall and good-looking his appearance was greeted with a low hum of admiration and anxiety. Half the audience had not known so grand a youth had lived among them. No wonder the princess loved him! What a terrible thing for him to be there!

As the youth advanced into the arena, he turned, as the custom was, to bow to the king: but he did not think at all of him; his eyes were fixed upon the princess, who sat to the right of her father. Had it not been for the barbaric part of her nature, it is probable that the lady would not have been there; but her intense soul would not allow her to be absent on an occasion in which she was so terribly interested. From the moment that the decree had gone forth, that her lover should decide his fate in the king's arena, she had thought of nothing, night or day, but this great event and the various subjects connected with it. With more power, influence, and force of character than any one who had ever before been interested in such a case, she had done what no other person had done – she had discovered the secret of the doors. She knew in which of the two rooms, that lay behind those doors, stood the tiger and in which one waited the lady. Through these thick doors, heavily curtained with skins on the inside, it was impossible that any noise or suggestion should come from within to the person who should approach to raise the latch of one of them; but gold, and the power of a woman's will, had brought the secret to the princess.

And not only did she know in which room stood the lady ready to emerge, all blushing and radiant, should her door be opened, but she knew who the lady was. It was one of the most beautiful maidens of the court who had been selected as a reward of the accused youth, should he be proved innocent of the crime of aspiring to one so far above him; and the princess hated her. Often had she seen, or imagined that she had seen, this attractive young woman throwing glances of admiration at her lover, and sometimes she thought these glances were appreciated and even returned. Now and then she had seen them talking together; it was but for a moment or two, but much can be said in a brief space; it may have been on most unimportant topics, but how could she know that? The girl was lovely, but she had dared to raise her eyes to the loved one of the princess; and, with all the intensity of her savage blood, she hated the woman who blushed and trembled behind that silent door.

When her lover turned and looked at her, and his eye met hers as she sat there paler and whiter than anyone in the vast crowd of anxious faces, he saw that she knew behind which door crouched the tiger, and behind which stood the lady. He had expected her to know it. He understood her nature, and he was sure that she would never rest until she had found out the secret.

Then it was that his quick and anxious glance asked the question: 'Which?' It was as plain to her as if he shouted it from where he stood. There was not an instant to be lost. The question was asked in a flash; it must be answered in another.

Her right arm lay on the cushioned parapet before her. She raised her hand and made a slight quick movement toward the right. No one but her lover saw her. Every eye but his was fixed on the man in the arena.

He turned, and with a firm and rapid step he walked across the empty space. Every heart stopped beating, every breath was held, every eye was fixed immovably upon that man. Without the slightest hesitation, he went to the door on the right and opened it.

Now, the point of the story is this. Did the tiger come out of that door, or did the lady?

Frank Stocton
(Adapted)

42

15
A Gude Buke

Ah like a gude buke
a buke's aw ye need
jis settle doon
hiv a right gude read

Ay, a gude buke's rerr
it makes ye think
nuthin tae beat it
bar a gude drink

Ah like a gude buke
opens yir mine
a gude companion
tae pass the time

See me wi a buke, bit
in a bus ur a train
canny whack it
wee wurld i yir ain

Ay, ah like a gude buke
widny deny it
dje know thon wan
noo – whit dje cry it?

Awright, pal, skip it
awright, keep the heid
howm ah tae know
yir tryin tae read?

Stephen Mulrine

16

A Good Poem

I like a good poem
one with lots of fighting
in it. Blood, and the
clanging of armour.   Poems

against Scotland are good,
and poems that defeat
the French with crossbows
I don't like poems that

aren't about anything.
Sonnets are wet and
a waste of time.
Also poems that don't

know how to rhyme.
If I was a poem
I'd play football and
get picked for England.

Roger McGough

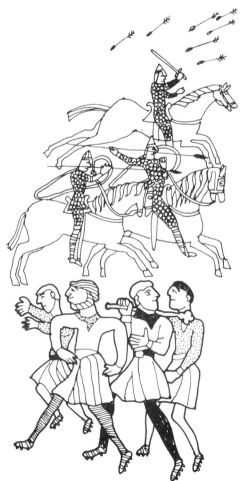

17
My Uncle Paul of Pimlico

My Uncle Paul of Pimlico
Has seven cats as white as snow,
Who sit at his enormous feet
And watch him, as a special treat,
Play the piano upside-down,
In his delightful dressing-gown;
The firelight leaps, the parlour glows,
And, while the music ebbs and flows,
They smile (while purring the refrains),
At little thoughts that cross their brains.

Mervyn Peake

18
The Ice-Cart

Perched on my city office-stool
I watched with envy while a cool
And lucky carter handled ice. . . .

And I was wandering in a trice
Far from the grey and grimy heat
Of that intolerable street
O'er sapphire berg and emerald floe
Beneath the still cold ruby glow
Of everlasting Polar night,
Bewildered by the queer half-light,
Until I stumbled unawares
Upon a creek where big white bears
Plunged headlong down with flourished heels
And floundered after shining seals
Through shivering seas of blinding blue
And, as I watched them, ere I knew,
I'd stripped and I was swimming too

Among the seal-pack, young and hale,
And thrusting on with threshing tail,
With twist and twirl and sudden leap
Through crackling ice and salty deep,
Diving and doubling with my kind
Until at last we left behind
Those big white blundering bulks of death,
And lay at length with panting breath
Upon a far untravelled floe
Beneath a gentle drift of snow –
Snow drifting gently fine and white
Out of the endless Polar night,
Falling and falling evermore
Upon that far untravelled shore
Till I was buried fathoms deep
Beneath that cold white drifting sleep –
Sleep drifting deep,
Deep drifting sleep. . . .

The carter cracked a sudden whip:
I clutched my stool with startled grip,
Awakening to the grimy heat
Of that intolerable street.

Wilfrid Gibson

19

Colonel Fazackerley

Colonel Fazackerley Butterworth-Toast
Bought an old castle complete with a ghost,
But someone or other forgot to declare
To Colonel Fazack that the spectre was there.

On the very first evening, while waiting to dine,
The Colonel was taking a fine sherry wine,
When the ghost, with a furious flash and a flare,
Shot out of the chimney and shivered, 'Beware!'

Colonel Fazackerley put down his glass
And said, 'My dear fellow, that's really first class!
I just can't conceive how you do it at all.
I imagine you're going to a Fancy Dress Ball?'

At this, the dread ghost gave a withering cry.
Said the Colonel (his monocle firm in his eye),
'Now just how you do it I wish I could think.
Do sit down and tell me, and please have a drink.'

The ghost in his phosphorous cloak gave a roar
And floated about between ceiling and floor.
He walked through a wall and returned through a pane
And backed up the chimney and came down again.

Said the Colonel, 'With laughter I'm feeling quite weak!'
(As trickles of merriment ran down his cheek).
'My house-warming party I hope you won't spurn.
You *must* say you'll come and you'll give us a turn!'

At this, the poor spectre – quite out of his wits –
Proceeded to shake himself almost to bits.
He rattled his chains and he clattered his bones
And he filled the whole castle with mumbles and moans.

But Colonel Fazackerley, just as before,
Was simply delighted and called out, 'Encore!'
At which the ghost vanished, his efforts in vain,
And never was seen at the castle again.

'Oh dear, what a pity!' said Colonel Fazack.
'I don't know his name, so I can't call him back.'
And then with a smile that was hard to define,
Colonel Fazackerley went in to dine.

Charles Causley

20

Ping-Pong

Swatted between bats
The celluloid ball
Leaps on unseen elastic
Skimming the taut net.

Sliced	Spun
Screwed	Cut
Dabbed	Smashed

Point
Service

Ping	Pong
Pong	Ping
Bing	Bong
Bong	Bing

Point
Service

Ding	Dong
Dong	Ding
Ting	Tong
Tang	Tong

Point
Service

Angled	Slipped
Cut	Driven
Floated	Caressed
Driven	Hammered

THWACKED
Point
Service

Bit	Bat
Tip	Tap
Slip	Slap
Zip	Zap
Whip	Whap

Point
Service

Left	Yes
Right	Yes

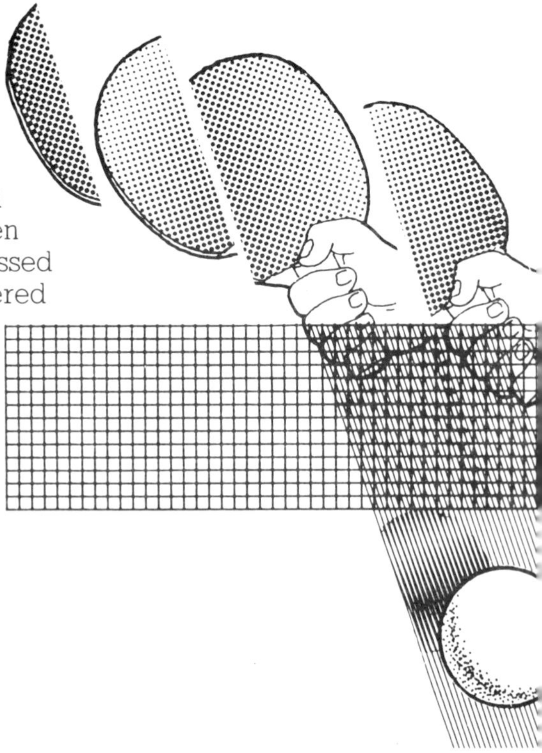

```
Twist          Yes
Skids               Yes
Eighteen     Seventeen
Eighteen       All
Nineteen             Eighteen
Nineteen       All
Twenty               Nineteen
        Point
        Service
Forehand     Backhand
Swerves      Yes
Rockets           Yes
Battered          Ah
Cracked           Ah
     SMASHED
        SMASHED
          SMASHED
      GAME.
```

Gareth Owen

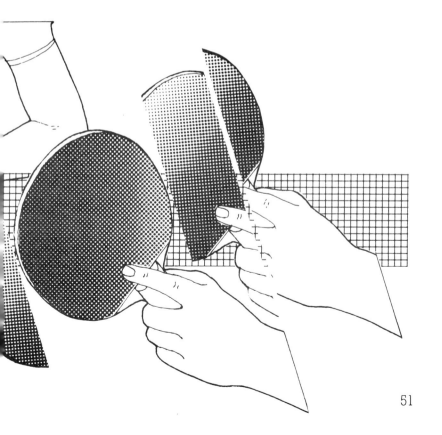

21
Special Days

How fast can your mother run? Could she keep up her speed and toss a pancake in a frying pan at the same time? If not, she needn't enter for a pancake race on Shrove Tuesday!

Shrove Tuesday is the day before Ash Wednesday, the day Lent begins. In the past, for the time between Ash Wednesday and Easter, Christians ate a very simple diet to commemorate Christ's fast in the wilderness. So, on Shrove Tuesday, thrifty housewives would use up all the food that wouldn't be allowed during Lent. Eggs, fat, flour and milk were mixed together and cooked over the fire in a frying pan. Because it was difficult to turn this floppy 'cake', it had to be tossed!

Shrove Tuesday, or Pancake Day, used to be a holiday, when Christians went to church to confess their sins before Lent began. When they had been forgiven, or shriven, they could enjoy the noisy sports such as bear-baiting or cock-fighting that would be going on in the streets. It would be the last opportunity for merrymaking before the quiet time of Lent.

On Shrove Tuesday, 1445, so the story goes, one woman of Olney was still cooking her pancakes when the 'shriving bell' rang to tell her to come to church. She grabbed her frying pan and, still wearing her apron, she ran to the church, tossing her pancake as she went.

In modern times, a pancake race is held in Olney on Shrove Tuesday. Only women can enter and the rules say that the pancake in each frying pan must still be cooking and must be tossed three times between the market square and the church. The prizes are a prayer book from the vicar and a kiss from the bell-ringer!

The fourth Sunday in Lent, usually around March 28, is Mothering Sunday. There's an old rhyme which says,

On Mothering Sunday above all other
Every child should dine with its mother.

Servant girls and apprentices learning their trades were allowed the day off to visit their mothers and they usually took a small gift with them – a posy of flowers or a cake.

A few days later, it's April Fool's Day. From dawn till noon on April 1, tricksters of all ages are at work. A victim could be told that a shoelace is undone and then be called an 'April Fool' for bending down to re-tie it; or a child might be sent to buy a left-handed screwdriver. In France, children make paper fish and try to fasten them on an adult's back without being seen.

There seems no special reason why April 1 should be chosen as a trick-playing day, but the idea of tricks and practical jokes is very old. Kings and noblemen used to have 'fools' or jesters at court or in their castles to tell jokes and keep them amused.

Anne Rigg

22

Children's Party

May I join you in the doghouse, Rover?
I wish to retire till the party's over.
Since three o'clock I've done my best
To entertain each tiny guest;
My conscience now I've left behind me,
And if they want me, let them find me.
I blew their bubbles, I sailed their boats,
I kept them from each other's throats.
I told them tales of magic lands,
I took them out to wash their hands.
I sorted their rubbers and tied their laces,
I wiped their noses and dried their faces.
Of similarity there's lots
'Twixt tiny tots and Hottentots.
I've earned repose to heal the ravages
Of these angelic-looking savages.
Oh, progeny playing by itself
Is a lonely fascinating elf,
But progeny in roistering batches
Would drive Saint Francis from here to Natchez.
Shunned are the games a parent proposes;
They prefer to squirt each other with hoses,
Their playmates are their natural foemen
And they like to poke each other's abdomen.
Their joy needs another's woe to cushion it,
Say a puddle, and somebody littler to push in it.
They observe with glee the ballistic results
Of ice cream with spoons for catapults,
And inform the assembly with tears and glares
That everyone's presents are better than theirs.
Oh, little women and little men,
Someday I hope to love you again,
But not till after the party's over,
So give me a key to the doghouse, Rover.

Ogden Nash

23
Bilbo's Party

The next day more carts rolled up the Hill, and still more carts. There might have been some grumbling about 'dealing locally', but that very week orders began to pour out of Bag End for every kind of provision, commodity, or luxury that could be obtained in Hobbiton or Bywater or anywhere in the neighbourhood. People became enthusiastic; and they began to tick off the days on the calendar; and they watched eagerly for the postman, hoping for invitations.

Before long the invitations began pouring out, and the Hobbiton post-office was blocked, and the Bywater post-office was snowed under, and voluntary assistant postmen were called for. There was a constant stream of them going up the Hill, carrying hundreds of polite variations on *Thank you, I shall certainly come.*

A notice appeared on the gate at Bag End: NO ADMITTANCE EXCEPT ON PARTY BUSINESS. Even those who had, or pretended to have Party Business were seldom allowed inside. Bilbo was busy: writing invitations, ticking off answers, packing up presents, and making some private preparations of his own. From the time of Gandalf's arrival he remained hidden from view.

One morning the hobbits woke to find the large field, south of Bilbo's front door, covered with ropes and poles for tents and pavilions. A special entrance was cut into the bank leading to the road, and wide steps and a large white gate were built there. The three hobbit-families of Bagshot Row, adjoining the field, were intensely interested and generally envied. Old Gaffer Gamgee stopped even pretending to work in his garden.

The tents began to go up. There was a specially large pavilion, so big that the tree that grew in the field was right inside it, and stood proudly near one end, at the head of the chief table. Lanterns were hung on all its branches. More promising still (to the hobbits' mind): an enormous open-air kitchen was erected in the north corner of the field. A draught of cooks, from every inn and eating-house for miles around, arrived to supplement the dwarves and other odd folk that were quartered at Bag End. Excitement rose to its height.

Then the weather clouded over. That was on Wednesday the

eve of the Party. Anxiety was intense. Then Thursday, September the 22nd, actually dawned. The sun got up, the clouds vanished, flags were unfurled and the fun began.

Bilbo Baggins called it a *party*, but it was really a variety of entertainments rolled into one. Practically everybody living near was invited. A very few were overlooked by accident, but as they turned up all the same, that did not matter. Many people from other parts of the Shire were also asked; and there were even a few from outside the borders. Bilbo met the guests (and additions) at the new white gate in person. He gave away presents to all and sundry – the latter were those who went out again by a back way and came in again by the gate. Hobbits give presents to other people on their own birthdays. Not very expensive ones, as a rule, and not so lavishly as on this occasion; but it was not a bad system. Actually in Hobbiton and Bywater every day in the year was somebody's birthday, so that every hobbit in those parts had a fair chance of at least one present at least once a week. But they never got tired of them.

On this occasion the presents were unusually good. The hobbit-children were so excited that for a while they almost forgot about eating. There were toys the like of which they had never seen before, all beautiful and some obviously magical. Many of them had indeed been ordered a year before, and had come all the way from the Mountain and from Dale, and were of real dwarf-make.

When every guest had been welcomed and was finally inside the gate, there were songs, dances, music, games, and, of course, food and drink. There were three official meals: lunch, tea, and dinner (or supper). But lunch and tea were marked chiefly by the fact that at those times all the guests were sitting down and eating together. At other times there were merely lots of people eating and drinking – continuously from elevenses until six-thirty, when the fireworks started.

The fireworks were by Gandalf: they were not only brought by him, but designed and made by him; and the special effects, set pieces, and flights of rockets were let off by him. But there was also a generous distribution of squibs, crackers, backarappers, sparklers, torches, dwarf-candles, elf-fountains, goblin-barkers and thunder-claps. They were all superb. The art of Gandalf improved with age.

There were rockets like a flight of scintillating birds singing with sweet voices. There were green trees with trunks of dark smoke: their leaves opened like a whole spring unfolding in a moment, and their shining branches dropped glowing flowers

down upon the astonished hobbits, disappearing with a sweet scent just before they touched their upturned faces. There were fountains of butterflies that flew glittering into the trees; there were pillars of coloured fires that rose and turned into eagles, or sailing ships, or a phalanx of flying swans; there was a red thunderstorm and a shower of yellow rain; there was a forest of silver spears that sprang suddenly into the air with a yell like an embattled army, and came down again into the Water with a hiss like a hundred hot snakes. And there was also one last surprise, in honour of Bilbo, and it startled the hobbits exceedingly, as Gandalf intended. The lights went out. A great smoke went up. It shaped itself like a mountain seen in the distance, and began to glow at the summit. It spouted green and scarlet flames. Out flew a red-golden dragon – not life-size, but terribly life-like: fire came from his jaws, his eyes glared down; there was a roar, and he whizzed three times over the heads of the crowd. They all ducked, and many fell flat on their faces. The dragon passed like an express train, turned a somersault, and burst over Bywater with a deafening explosion.

'That is the signal for supper!' said Bilbo. The pain and alarm vanished at once, and the prostrate hobbits leaped to their feet. There was a splendid supper for everyone; for everyone, that is, except those invited to the special family dinner-party. This was held in the great pavilion with the tree. The invitations were limited to twelve dozen (a number also called by the hobbits one Gross, though the word was not considered proper to use of people); and the guests were selected from all the families to which Bilbo and Frodo were related, with the addition of a few special unrelated friends (such as Gandalf). Many young hobbits were included, and present by parental permission; for hobbits were easy-going with their children in the matter of sitting up late, especially when there was a chance of getting them a free meal. Bringing up young hobbits took a lot of provender.

There were many Bagginses and Boffins, and also many Tooks and Brandybucks; there were various Grubbs (relations of Bilbo Baggins' grandmother), and various Chubbs (connexions of his Took grandfather); and a selection of Burrowses, Bolgers, Bracegirdles, Brockhouses, Goodbodies, Hornblowers and Proudfoots. Some of these were only very distantly connected with Bilbo, and some had hardly ever been in Hobbiton before, as they lived in remote corners of the Shire. The Sackville-Bagginses were not forgotten. Otho and his wife Lobelia were present. They disliked Bilbo and detested Frodo, but so magnificent was the invitation card, written in golden ink, that they had felt it was impossible to refuse. Besides, their cousin, Bilbo, had been specializing in food for many years and his table had a high reputation.

All the one hundred and forty-four guests expected a pleasant feast; though they rather dreaded the after-dinner speech of their host (an inevitable item). He was liable to drag in bits of what he called poetry; and sometimes, after a glass or two, would allude to the absurd adventures of his mysterious journey. The guests were not disappointed: they had a *very* pleasant feast, in fact an engrossing entertainment: rich, abundant, varied, and prolonged. The purchase of provisions fell almost to nothing throughout the district in the ensuing weeks; but as Bilbo's catering had depleted the stocks of most of the stores, cellars and warehouses for miles around, that did not matter much.

After the feast (more or less) came the Speech. Most of the company were, however, now in a tolerant mood, at that delightful stage which they called 'filling up the corners'. They were sipping their favourite drinks, and nibbling at their favourite dainties, and their fears were forgotten. They were prepared to listen to anything, and to cheer at every full stop.

My dear people, began Bilbo, rising in his place. 'Hear! Hear! Hear!' they shouted, and kept on repeating it in chorus, seeming reluctant to follow their own advice. Bilbo left his place and went and stood on a chair under the illuminated tree. The light of the lanterns fell on his beaming face; the golden buttons shone on his embroidered silk waistcoat. They could all see him standing, waving one hand in the air, the other was in his trouser-pocket.

My dear Bagginses and Boffins, he began again; *and my dear Tooks and Brandybucks, and Grubbs, and Chubbs, and Burrowses, and Hornblowers, and Bolgers, Bracegirdles, Goodbodies, Brockhouses and Proudfoots*. 'ProudFEET!' shouted an elderly hobbit from the back of the pavilion. His name, of course, was Proudfoot, and well merited; his feet were large, exceptionally furry, and both were on the table.

Proudfoots, repeated Bilbo. *Also my good Sackville-Bagginses that I welcome back at last to Bag End. Today is my one hundred and eleventh birthday: I am eleventy-one today!* 'Hurray! Hurray! Many Happy Returns!' they shouted, and they hammered joyously on the tables. Bilbo was doing splendidly. This was the sort of stuff they liked: short and obvious.

I hope you are all enjoying yourselves as much as I am. Deafening cheers. Cries of *Yes* (and *No*). Noises of trumpets and horns, pipes and flutes, and other musical instruments. There were, as has been said, many young hobbits present. Hundreds of musical crackers had been pulled. Most of them bore the mark DALE on them; which did not convey much to most of the hobbits, but they all agreed they were marvellous crackers. They contained instruments, small, but of perfect make and enchanting tones. Indeed, in one corner some of the young Tooks and Brandybucks, supposing Uncle Bilbo to have finished (since he had plainly said all that was necessary), now got up an impromptu orchestra, and began a merry dance-tune. Master Everard Took and Miss Melilot Brandybuck got on a table and with bells in their hands began to dance the Springle-ring: a pretty dance, but rather vigorous.

J. R. R. Tolkien

24

False Security

I remember the dread with which I at a quarter past four
Let go with a bang behind me our house front door
And, clutching a present for my dear little hostess tight,
Sailed out for the children's party into the night
Or rather the gathering night. For still some boys
In the near municipal acres were making a noise
Shuffling in fallen leaves and shouting and whistling
And running past hedges of hawthorn, spiky and bristling.
And black in the oncoming darkness stood out the trees
And pink shone the ponds in the sunset ready to freeze
And all was still and ominous waiting for dark
And the keeper was ringing his closing bell in the park
And the arc lights started to fizzle and burst into mauve
As I climbed West Hill to the great big house in The Grove,
Where the children's party was and the dear little hostess.
But halfway up stood the empty house where the ghost is.
I crossed to the other side and under the arc
Made a rush for the next kind lamp-post out of the dark
And so to the next and the next till I reached the top
Where The Grove branched off to the left. Then ready to drop
I ran to the ironwork gateway of number seven
Secure at last on the lamplit fringe of Heaven.
Oh who can say how subtle and safe one feels
Shod in one's children's sandals from Daniel Neal's,
Clad in one's party clothes made of stuff from Heal's?
And who can still one's thrill at the candle shine
On cakes and ices and jelly and blackcurrant wine,
And the warm little feel of my hostess's hand in mine?
Can I forget my delight at the conjuring show?
And wasn't I proud that I was the last to go?
Too overexcited and pleased with myself to know
That the words I heard my hostess's mother employ
To a guest departing, would ever diminish my joy,
I WONDER WHERE JULIA FOUND THAT STRANGE, RATHER
COMMON LITTLE BOY?

John Betjeman

25

Hallowe'en

When I was a wee girl in Glasgow, Hallowe'en was celebrated by all of us with keenest enjoyment. The weather always seemed clear and frosty, the skies filled with stars, and there was the exhilaration of dressing up in strange garments, with the added tension and nervousness of a performance about to begin. I usually wore Grannie's old hat, when it had got beyond the stage when a bunch of cherries or a spray of flowers could rejuvenate it, and I sat it on top of my head at a rakish angle, over my blackened face. A long skirt of my mother's, and Grannie's tartan shawl completed the disguise, but I wasn't able to round off the effect with my mother's high-heeled shoes because I couldn't even hobble in them, so my long-legged boots and black woollen stockings just had to be worn, even though they were completely out of character. This was a terrible disappointment, for I longed to prance about in elegant high heels, but for running out and in closes and up and down dozens of stairs sure footing was vital, and boots it had to be.

There was much giggling and mutual admiration when we all met after tea, and set out on the rounds of all the neighbours' houses. Sometimes, greatly daring, we went beyond our own district, and we shivered with excitement, and a little dread at the thought of knocking at such strange doors. We were very critical of the brasses, and surprised to find that in some posh closes the name-plates weren't a patch on the glittering gold polish our own mothers managed. We each carried a little bag, home-made from an old petticoat or blouse, with a draw-string top, to hold the expected apples and nuts and sweets we hoped we would collect, and we prepared our acts as we raced along from close to close. We never expected to be handed our Hallowe'en gifts just for knocking on a door and chanting, 'Please gi'e us wur Hallowe'en!* We knew we were expected to do a turn to entertain our benefactors.

We would be invited into the house, and the family would sit round in lively anticipation as we went into our performances. I usually sang the latest popular song, and I particularly liked one requiring the use of my hostess's fluebrush, which I stuck over

---

* *gi'e us wur*: give us our.

my shoulder and used as a bayonet. Very dashing I thought this, and so did my audience! There were recitations and ballads, and we generally finished with all of us doing a Highland Fling. We received our applause with flushed and happy faces, and we opened our draw-string bags to receive the apples, and the nuts, with maybe a piece of puff candy or some home-made tablet. Tablet was a great treat and so tempting that it was devoured on the spot, and seldom rested in the bag for a second. A turnip lantern lit our way and we went bobbing through the darkness like glow-worms. The preparation of those magic lanterns was a great ploy. We hollowed out swede turnips skilfully, made two slits for the eyes and a perpendicular line for the nose. A curved slit made a smiling mouth. A little hollow in the bottom held our candle, and the complete effect was golden

and delightful. I may say everybody in our district ate mashed swedes for days afterwards, using up the discarded insides of our lanterns.

A party was a great excitement at Hallowe'en, and everyone went in fancy dress. Home-made, of course, for these were unsophisticated as well as hard-up days, and only 'toffs' would have known about hiring clothes. Angels and fairies, their wings fashioned from cardboard boxes coaxed from the Cooperative, and covered with coloured crinkled paper, were ten a penny, for the girls. The boys favoured pirates and cowboys, which were easily fashioned from old hats, and their father's leather belts, and toy guns. All this helped to break down the shyness we would have felt in ordinary clothes, although Hallowe'en fun was so different from any other form of merriment there was never a minute of sitting still wondering what you were expected to do. After the tea, with its salmon sandwiches if we were lucky, or corn mutton if money was tight, followed by the jellies, the games started. The big zinc bath was pulled from under the bed and filled with cold water, then rosy-cheeked apples were tumbled in in a colourful shower. A chair was placed with its back to the bath, the apples and water given a vigorous stir to send them bobbing as wildly as possible and make a difficult target, and we would each kneel, one at a time, on the chair, head sticking out over the top edge just as though we were about to be guillotined. A fork was held between clenched teeth, and we'd gaze at the bobbing fruit below us, waiting for the moment when the biggest and reddest apple was exactly placed for our aim, then *plonk*, down went the fork, usually to slither off between the bouncing apples. There would be howls of glee from the onlookers, and gulping disappointment from the unlucky contestant as he or she climbed down from the chair to go to the end of the queue again. Not till everybody had speared an apple would the next game start, and, of course, it became harder and harder to succeed as the numbers of apples grew fewer and fewer with each win, and the final apple had the whole room shouting opposite advice.

There was a lovely game, unpopular with parents but beloved by us children, where a huge home-baked soda scone was covered in treacle and suspended on a string from the centre gas bracket, or hung from a string stretched across the room. It was sent spinning by the leader, and then, with hands clasped behind our backs, we would leap into the air and try to snatch a bite. What a glorious mess we were in at the end of the caper, hair, eyes, cheeks and neck covered in treacle. Mothers and aunties and uncles urged us instantly towards the kitchen sink, 'Go and dicht yer faces noo, we don't want treacle a' ower the hoose,' and what a splashing there was under the cold tap, and a battle for the solitary towel as we removed the mess.

And, of course, we loved the trinkets which were buried in a mound of creamy mashed potatoes. Even the poorest family could afford tatties, so everybody could enjoy this traditional bit of fun. The quantities of potato we consumed in search of our favourite ring or threepenny piece must have saved many an anxious hostess from worrying how she was to fill us up.

The older girls were full of romantic notions concerning apples. They'd try to take off the peel in one continuous strand, which they threw over their left shoulder, and whichever initial it formed was supposed to be that of the lad they would marry. Oh the teasing and the blushing if by chance the initial formed was that of their current heart-throb. The boys pretended they had no interest in this performance, but there was plenty of jeering and pushing when the initial fitted, and a casual pairing off when the game had finished. Especially if the next game was the one where an apple was placed on the top edge of a door, with a chair placed on either side, a boy on one chair and a girl on the other. They each ate towards the core, and the winners were the couple who reached the core – and a kiss – in the shortest possible time.

We children thought the swinging apple game was far better, and it was funnier too. There were up to six contestants at a time required for this game, which made it rare and noisy and exciting. They had to stand in line, in front of six apples suspended on cords from a string stretched across the room. The apples were set swinging, and the point of the game was that, without using hands to help, the contestants had to bite the fruit right down to the core. The winner, of course, was the one who finished first. The apple could be manoeuvred on to one shoulder only *once* during the game to assist the eating, but otherwise everybody leaped and bit like hungry birds, and a most comical sight it was for the onlookers. It was especially funny when the grown-ups took their turn, and we held our sides with laughter when specs slithered down perspiring noses, when braces parted from buttons, and when false teeth were dislodged on hitting an apple too suddenly. We could have played this game all night, but all at once the apples were finished, and it was time to go home, this time without lanterns to light our way, for, of course, we didn't take them to parties, only when we went out chanting 'Please gi'e us wur Hallowe'en'.

Molly Weir

26

Tinsel

Joe was having his tea and Jim felt like staying in and Annie's mother wouldn't let her out.

He stood on the pavement outside the paper-shop, peering in through the lighted window at the Christmas annuals and selection boxes. The queue for the evening papers reached right to the door of the shop. The snow on the pavement was packed hard and grey-brown, yellow in places under the streetlamps. He scraped at the snow with the inside of his boot, trying to rake up enough to make a snowball, but it was too powdery and it clung to the fingers of his woollen gloves, making his hands feel clogged and uncomfortable. He took off his gloves and scooped up some slush from the side of the road but the cold made his bare fingers sting, red. It felt as if he'd just been belted by Miss Heather.

Annie's big brother Tommy was clattering his way across the road, trailing behind him a sack full of empty bottles. He'd gathered them on the terracing at Ibrox and he was heading for the Family Department of the pub to cash in as many as he could. Every time the pub door opened the noise and light seeped out. It was a bit like pressing your hands over your ears then easing off then pressing again. If you did that again and again people's voices sounded like mwah ... mwah ... mwah ... mwah. ...

He looked closely at the snow still clogging his gloves. It didn't look at all like the crystals in his book. Disgusted, he slouched towards his close.

Going up the stairs at night he always scurried or charged past each closet for fear of what might be lurking there ready to leap out at him. Keeping up his boldness, he whistled loudly. Little Star of Bethlehem. He was almost at the top when he remembered the decorations.

*   *   *

The kitchen was very bright after the dimness of the landing with its sputtering gas light.

'Nob'dy wis comin out tae play,' he explained.

His mother wiped her hands. 'Right! What about these decorations!'

The decorations left over from last year were in a cardboard box under the bed. He didn't like it under there. It was dark and dirty, piled with old rubbish – books, clothes, boxes, tins. Once he'd crawled under looking for a comic, dust choking him, and he'd scuttled back in horror from bugs and darting silverfish. Since then he'd had bad dreams about the bed swarming with insects that got into his mouth when he tried to breathe.

His father rummaged in the sideboard drawer for a packet of tin tacks and his mother brought out the box.

Streamers and a few balloons and miracles of coloured paper that opened out into balls or long concertina snakes. On the table his mother spread out some empty cake boxes she'd brought home from work and cut them into shapes like Christmas trees and bells, and he got out his painting box and a saucerful of water and he coloured each one and left it to dry – green for the trees and yellow for the bells, the nearest he could get to gold.

His father had bought something special.

'Jist a wee surprise. It wis only a coupla coppers in Woollies.'

From a cellophane bag he brought out a length of shimmering rustling silver.

'What dis that say daddy?' He pointed at the label.

'It says UNTARNISHABLE TINSEL GARLAND.'

'What dis that mean?'

'Well that's what it is. It's a tinsel garland. Tinsel's the silvery stuff it's made a. An a garland's jist a big long sorta decoration, for hangin up. An untarnishable means ... well ... how wid ye explain it hen?'

'Well,' said his mother, 'it jist means it canny get wasted. It always steys nice an shiny.'

'Aw Jesus!' said his father. 'Ther's only three tacks left!'

'Maybe the paper-shop'll be open.'

'It wis open a wee minnit ago!'

'Ah'll go an see,' said his father, putting on his coat and scarf. 'Shouldnae be very long.'

*   *   *

The painted cut-out trees and bells had long since dried and still his father hadn't come back. His mother had blown up the balloons and she'd used the three tacks to put up some streamers. Then she remembered they had a roll of sticky tape. It was more awkward to use than the tacks so the job took a little longer. But gradually the room was transformed, brightened; magical colours strung across the ceiling. A game he liked to play was lying on his back looking up at the ceiling and trying to imagine it was actually the floor and the whole room was upside down. When he did it now it looked like a toy garden full of swaying paper plants.

Round the lampshade in the centre of the room his mother was hanging the tinsel coil, standing on a chair to reach up. When she'd fixed it in place she climbed down and stood back and they watched the swinging lamp come slowly to rest. Then they looked at each other and laughed.

When they heard his father's key in the door his mother shooshed and put out the light. They were going to surprise him. He came in and fumbled for the switch. They were laughing and when he saw the decorations he smiled but he looked bewildered and a bit sad.

He put the box of tacks on the table.

'So ye managed, eh,' he said. He smiled again, his eyes still sad. 'Ah'm sorry ah wis so long. The paper-shop wis shut an ah had tae go down nearly tae Govan Road.'

Then they understood. He was sad because they'd done it all without him. Because they hadn't waited. They said nothing. His mother filled the kettle. His father took off his coat.

'Time you were in bed malad!' he said.

'Aw bit daddy, themorra's Sunday!'

'Bed!'

'Och!'

He could see it was useless to argue so he washed his hands and face and put on the old shirt he slept in.

'Mammy, ah need a pee.'

Rather than make him get dressed again to go out and down the stairs, she said he could use the sink. She turned on the tap and lifted him up to kneel on the ledge.

When he pressed his face up close to the window he could see the back court lit here and there by the light from a window, shining out on to the yellow snow from the dark bulk of the tenements. There were even one or two Christmas trees and, up above, columns of pale grey smoke, rising from chimneys. When he leaned back he could see the reflection of their own kitchen. He imagined it was another room jutting out beyond the window, out into the dark. He could see the furniture, the curtain across the bed, his mother and father, the decorations and through it all, vaguely, the buildings, the night. And hung there, shimmering, in that room he could never enter, the tinsel garland that would never ever tarnish.

Alan Spence

27

There are no Lights on Our Christmas Tree

The time has come for festivities
For party games and revelries
As I was walking home the other night
I heard a little voice so clear and bright

CHORUS
There are no lights on our Christmas tree
We must not spoil Dad's telly V
No party games, no mistletoe
Just whisper Wenceslas and out you go.

Just once a year I like to be a square
I love to feel the tinsel in my hair
I love to hear the songs of days gone by
But dad and me we don't see eye to eye.

The box of crackers from our Uncle Alf
Lies un-opened on the shelf
Dad has forbidden but we're hoping he
Won't notice one more bang in Laramie

When I grow up to be a man
There'll be no television in my plan
With joy and laughter my house will ring
I never want to hear my children sing

Cyril Tawney

28

Kidnapped at Christmas

Two men, Gilbert and Crosby, are spending Christmas in prison. Gilbert is sitting on a chair, reading a comic. Crosby is lying on his top bunk bed, restless.

GILBERT *(singing)*: Good King Wenceslas knocked a bobby senseless, right in the middle of Marks and Spencers...

CROSBY: *Shut up!*

GILBERT: Sorry. *(Pause)* Good King Wenceslas looked out, of his bedroom winder, when a poor man came in sight, he gave him a red-hot cinder...

CROSBY: *Shut up!*

GILBERT: I'm only trying to cheer us up, Crosby.

CROSBY: Don't bother. *(Getting up)* This is no place to be at Christmas, this is no place to be at all! Shall I tell you something, Gilbert? This is the worst possible place to be on Christmas Eve, bar none.

GILBERT: Shall I sing, While shepherds watched their turnip tops?

CROSBY: No! You know where we should be tonight, don't you? Out there – doing evil things. Sawing down the Christmas Tree in Trafalgar Square; chucking a brick through a toy-shop window; mugging carol singers. All like that. This could be the best night of the year for us, and where are we?

In flippin' clink.

GILBERT: Chicken dinner tomorrow, Crosby, and Christmas pud.

CROSBY: Chicken dinner? Chicken dinner? I don't want no chicken dinner. Not *prison* chicken dinner, all cold and greasy; horrible clammy sprouts, lumpy mashed spuds, greasy gravy. I want my freedom, matey, that's what I want. I want to enjoy myself. What prison are we in?

GILBERT: Maximum security.

CROSBY: I thought we must be. I thought they'd put us in with a load of rascals and villains. *(Gazing at the audience)* Look at 'em! Did you ever see such a collection of rogues and vagabonds? Fancy being stuck here over Christmas with all them ugly-mugs staring at you.

GILBERT *(studies the audience, then)*: The little one's aren't too bad, Crosby, it's the big ones that are ugly. Some of the little ones don't look all that bad at all.

CROSBY: They all look horrible. Horrible. I'll tell you, matey, I've been in a lot of nicks: Dartmoor, the Ville, Wormwood Scrubs, but I've never before been locked up with a bunch as ugly as this lot here. Never. And it's fizzin' Christmas Eve, would you believe? What are this lot in for? Frightening babies?

GILBERT: They're the audience.

CROSBY: They're still horrible.

GILBERT: Mums and dads and kids. They could help us to escape.

CROSBY: Escape?

GILBERT: Yes.

CROSBY: Tonight?

GILBERT: Yes.

CROSBY: Do you think they would?

GILBERT: I don't know. If you stop calling them names they might. If you could try and be a bit more *nice* to them.

Crosby thinks it over, then adopts an ingratiating smile.

CROSBY: Hello, Kiddies! Hello, little children! Hello mums and dads! Are you all enjoying yourselves – I hope so. 'Cos if you're not enjoying yourselves, I'll break out of here, be in them stalls like a dose of salts, and I'll duff up the lot of you!

GILBERT: Is that the nicest you can be?

CROSBY: Not nice enough?

GILBERT: Nowhere near. They're hardly likely to help us, are they, if you talk to them like that.

CROSBY: I'll try again. Hello, Kiddiewinkies! Are all the good children sitting comfortably? Who's going to help their nice kind Uncle Crosby get out of the nasty cruel prison then? Did I hear somebody say 'not me'? Did one of you horrible monsters say 'not me'? My life, I'll be over the end of that stage and clipping earholes faster than you can say hard labour!

Remembering himself, he glances guiltily at Gilbert who shakes his head.

CROSBY: Let me have another try. Let's find out how many of these lovely boys and girls are going to help us to escape. All the ones who are going to help us get out of this prison, raise your right hands. High up in the air. Now, all the ones who want us to stay locked up, raise your left hands. Right – all the ones with their right hands in the air, turn round and duff up all of them with their left hands up.

GILBERT: No, no, no, no! That's no good either.

CROSBY: I've got another one. Hands up all the little boys and girls who came in daddy's car this afternoon? Mummy's car? If you came on the bus or the tube, stick your hands in your pockets and keep shtum. Only those who came in a motor-car with daddy or mummy put their hands up. Good. Now I want you to slip your hand, nicely and gently, into daddy's pocket or mummy's handbag and nick the car keys.

GILBERT: That's worse than ever.

CROSBY: I don't see why. If we're going to make a quick getaway we're going to need some wheels.

GILBERT: I've got a better idea. Can you all shout out loud? Can you shout, 'Your shoe-lace is undone'? Again. And every time I scratch my nose, I want to hear you shout, 'Your shoe-lace is undone'. Shall we try it? *(He scratches his nose)* Again. *(He scratches his nose again)* Very good.

CROSBY: Aren't you going to fasten it?

GILBERT: Fasten what?

CROSBY: Your shoe-lace?

GILBERT: What shoe-lace?

CROSBY: The one that's undone.

GILBERT: It isn't undone.

CROSBY: It isn't mine is it?

GILBERT: Nobody's shoe-lace is undone. It's all part of the plan. To escape. With their help. Listen to this, and tell me what you think. I create a fuss – we both kick up a fuss. We start shouting and screaming until the warder comes. He says, 'Why are you kicking up a fuss?' He says, 'What are you shouting and screaming about?' We say, 'Help us, save us, save us! There's a big hairy spider climbing up the wall...'

CROSBY: Where? Where is it? I'll smash it! I'll stamp on it! I'll spifflicate it! I hate spiders – horrible hairy things!

GILBERT: There isn't really a spider. That's just what we tell him. We make the spider up. The warder comes into our cell. He gets out his truncheon to bash the spider with. I scratch my nose. Like this. They shout, 'Your shoe-lace is undone'. The warder gives you his truncheon to hold while he bends down to tie up his shoe. Then, while he's bending down, you bop him on the nut.

CROSBY: With his truncheon.

GILBERT: Yes.

CROSBY: Great, Gilbert!

GILBERT: Do you really like it?

CROSBY: Fantastic. I hate warders. I hate warders more than anything. I'll give it to him, wham-bam, right on his head. Great.

GILBERT: Not too hard though.

CROSBY: Just hard enough.

GILBERT: Off we go then.

The pair of them start to scream and shout and generally kick up a fuss. Warder Mullins enters.

MULLINS: Orlright, orlright – knock it off. There's quite a number of respectable convicts in here trying to get some sleep.

GILBERT ⎱
CROSBY ⎰ : Help! Help! Save us! Save us!

MULLINS: What's it all in aid of anyway? Why are you kicking up a fuss? What's all this shouting and screaming about?

GILBERT ⎱ .Oh, help us, Warder Mullins! Save us! There's a great
CROSBY ⎰ 'big hairy spider climbing up the wall of our cell!

MULLINS: Are you sure?

GILBERT: Its legs are that long!

CROSBY: It's all hairy and horrible, Warder Mullins!

MULLINS: Let's have a look.

The warder produces an impressive key, unlocks the door, and enters the cell. He produces his truncheon.

MULLINS: Whereabouts is it?

GILBERT: Over there.

Gilbert scratches his nose, but when the audience call out, 'Your shoe-lace is undone', it is Crosby who bends down to investigate his footwear.

MULLINS: Come on – where is it?

Gilbert behind the warder's back, makes elaborate gestures at Crosby who gets the message.

GILBERT: Hang on, Warder, I've lost it now – I'll look again.

Gilbert scratches his nose again. The audience call out again. Crosby waits gleefully for the warder to react, but again the warder doesn't move. The ritual is gone through yet again.

MULLINS: Well? Where's this horrible hairy spider? I'm still waiting, both of you! If this is your idea of a joke . . .

GILBERT: Excuse me, Warder, but I think your shoe-lace is undone.

CROSBY: I'll hold your truncheon for you if you like while you tie it up again.

MULLINS *(without looking down)*: Not my shoe-lace. I never use them. I wear special-issue prison-officer heavy-duty elastic-sided boots. Now then, where's this horrible hairy spider?

GILBERT: I can't see it now. It must have gone away, Mr Mullins.

But as Gilbert is speaking, a horrible hairy spider descends from above, unnoticed by Gilbert and Crosby. The enormous spider terrifies the Warder who quakes in his elastic-sided boots, and then bolts, slamming the cell door behind him. The spider disappears again.

CROSBY: It didn't work, did it?

GILBERT: Not quite.

CROSBY: We'll be stuck in here all over Christmas. For prison chicken dinner and it'll be all slimy and greasy, with clammy sprouts, lumpy spuds and greasy gravy.

GILBERT: Perhaps it won't be all that bad.

CROSBY: It'll be horrible, No crackers – they don't have crackers.

I hate not having crackers. I'll probably end up throwing clammy sprouts at one of the warders, then they'll put me into solitary confinement. I'll tell you something else as well.

GILBERT: What's that?

CROSBY: My shoe-lace *is* undone.

GILBERT: What do you want me to do about it?

CROSBY: I was wondering if you would tie it up for me? I can't do double bows. I *hate* double-bows. I can do single bows but they're always coming loose. And if I tie knots I can never undo them.

GILBERT: Give us your foot.

As Gilbert is tying Crosby's shoe, the horrible hairy spider descends again. Gilbert sees it first, and reacts with horror. Crosby follows his glance. They dash for the cell door - and find it unlocked. Once they are out on the other side, they react with surprise.

CROSBY: We're out!

GILBERT: He forgot to lock it!

CROSBY: We're free!

GILBERT: Very nearly. Come on, let's make a dash for it.

But as they cross the stage, the Warder returns with Warder MacBain. The Warders carry guns and have come in pursuit of the spider, which has vanished again. Crosby and Gilbert duck into the shadows as the two Warders approach the empty cell, cautiously. The Warders peer up towards the ceiling.

MACBAIN: Are you sure you're not having me on, Mr Mullins?

MULLINS: Have I ever lied to you, Mr MacBain?

MACBAIN: No, but you have been known to exaggerate slightly.

MULLINS: Not this time - it was enormous. *And* horrible *and* hairy.

MACBAIN: You're sure you haven't been treating yourself to an unofficial glassful of the Governor's Christmas Day medium-dry sherry?

MULLINS: All right then - don't believe me. Don't take my word for it. I wasn't the only one that saw the spider. Gilbert and Crosby saw it first - they shouted for me to come and look at it. *(He looks down at the lower half of the cell and is immediately suspicious)* Hang on! Hold up!

MACBAIN: What is it now - I suppose you've seen a six foot cockroach?

MULLINS: Not at all. Do me a favour, would you? Check the contents of this cell. Just go over the inventory in your head and tell me if you notice anything untoward or missing?

MACBAIN: No – not on a cursory inspection. Two beds, convicts for the use of, two chairs, similar, one table, two little enamelled potties ... Wait a minute, now that you come to mention it – there's two convicts missing!

Warder Mullins tries the cell door and finds it unlocked.

MULLINS: They've done a bunk! Convicts Gilbert and Crosby have hopped it!

At which point, Gilbert and Crosby break from cover in the shadows and seek refuge in the audience. The two Warders produce whistles, blow short sharp blasts, and pursue the convicts in a wild chase around the auditorium. At the end of the chase we have lost both the convicts and the warders.

A Detective, Grummett, enters and addresses the audience.

GRUMMETT: Right then – nobody move! My name is Detective Constable Stephen Grummett, C.I.D., and it is my duty to tell you that nobody will be allowed to leave this auditorium, not even to get a tub of chocolate ice-cream or to go to the lavvy. Two convicts, Crosby and Gilbert, have made their escape from off this stage and it's believed that the breakout took place with the assistance of a person or persons unknown, most probably a member or members of this audience. During the next two hours, I shall pass among you all taking the names and addresses of every man, woman, boy and girl sitting out there. In order not to cause you too much inconvenience, it has been decided to allow the play to continue up here, while I'm out there. And I look forward to receiving the maximum co-operation from you all. The sooner we get everything cleared up, the sooner we can all go home. I shall be commencing my enquiries about there – *(He waves towards the back of the Stalls)* – somewhere. I do have my eye on a particularly suspicious-looking male parent in Row 'M'. Yes, sir, you, sir, you know who I mean. The gentleman in the brown suit with the glasses and the bag of liquorice all-sorts. I'm on my way to join you – and it's to be hoped that the child that is with you can offer a reasonable explanation for your being here.

The Detective goes off.

Willis Hall

29

The Fortress

It was Christmas Eve and getting dark, with quick flurries of snow on the east wind. Chas and Clogger were in the Crow's Nest. Chas was wearing his suede jerkin and a bright red steel helmet marked *Caparetto* in fairly-neat white lettering. Clogger was wearing his boy scout uniform and another bright red helmet, also marked *Caparetto.*

Chas was very uncomfortable; the wind made his eyes water, and the iron-hard chin-strap of the old helmet was cutting into his chin.

The Crow's Nest was well made of Royal Navy packing-cases and perched in the highest tree. It had a roof of Fish Quay Buster, that rippled like thunder in the wind.

Clogger swept the horizon again, with the great brass telescope that had belonged to Captain Nichol.

'Nothing in sight, sir. He'll no come tonight. Visibility's down to a hundred yards and ma auntie'll be mad if A'm not home for tea soon.'

'O.K. Stand down, Petty Officer.' They climbed stiffly down the rope ladder, manhandling the telescope between them, and wriggled into Fortress Caparetto. It was great in the Fortress. The Quartermaster-cook had the kettle nearly boiling on the paraffin-heater, and the long Anderson shelter was as warm as toast. You could *make* toast on the paraffin-heater, if you were patient enough. It took half-an-hour, and it was hard to tell if the dark patches were toasting or soot; but it tasted hot and fine, spread with plenty of butter from the seven-pound tin. Clogger said the tin of butter would keep for ages in this cold weather.

Sergeant Jones, Private Nichol and Corporal Carstairs (otherwise known as Carrot-juice) lounged on the pink-sprigged mattresses that covered the bunks, staring at the candle-flames and waiting for their brew, as content as cats. There was nowhere as safe as Fortress Caparetto in the whole of Garmouth. Above the thin steel of the Anderson's arched roof were three solid feet of earth and rockery, concreted together here and there. It would have withstood anything but a direct hit from the *Bismarck.* An old patchwork quilt kept draughts from the door. Beyond, lay the machine-gun emplacement, walled with pongy sandbags and floored with a framework of boards.

Chas's heart glowed with pride. All done in a fortnight and as dry as a bone, thanks to the Fish Quay Buster. And the Quartermaster, she kept it so *neat* with rows of shining white mugs, red firebuckets brimming with sand, red helmets hanging on the wall and a notice-board marked *Fortress Caparetto – Standing Orders.* Chas was not quite sure what Standing Orders were, so they were read out twice a day, with everybody standing up respectfully.

1. Anyone who steals food from the Fortress, if found guilty by Court Martial, shall be thrown in the goldfish pond. They may take off any clothes they want to first, but Keep It Decent.
2. Anyone touching the Gun without permission will be chucked out of the Fortress for Three Months. Anyone who speaks to Boddser Brown for any reason will be chucked out for Good.
3. Anyone lying on the bunks will tidy up afterwards.
4. No peeing within fifty yards, or Anything Else.
5. Always come in by the back fence, after making sure you're not followed.
6. No stealing from shops without permission. All goods stolen belong to the Fortress.
7. Only sentries will touch the air-rifle. Hand back all pellets out of your pockets etc when coming off duty.
8. Do not mess about with catapults inside the Fortress or you will wash up for four days.
9. Do not mess about at all.
10. Penalty for splitting to parents, teachers etc is DEATH.
11. Do not waste anything.
12. Anyone who brings in useless old junk will take it back to the Tip where they got it.
13. Quartermaster gives out all the eats. Don't argue with her.

After the orders had been read out, everyone bent and swore to keep them, with their hands on the machine-gun.

Robert Westall

30

The Ants at the Olympics

At last year's Jungle Olympics,
the Ants were completely outclassed.
In fact, from an entry of sixty-two teams,
the Ants came their usual last.

They didn't win one single medal.
Not that that's a surprise.
The reason was not for lack of trying
but more their unfortunate size.

While the cheetahs won most of the sprinting
And the hippos won putting the shot,
the Ants tried sprinting but couldn't
and tried to put but could not.

It was sad for the Ants 'cause they're sloggers.
They turn out for every event
With their shorts and their bright orange tee-shirts,
their athletes are proud they are sent.

They came last at the high jump and hurdles,
which they say they'd have won, but they fell.
They came last in the four hundred metres
and last in the swimming as well.

They came last in the long-distance running,
though they say they might have come first.
And they might if the other sixty-one teams
Hadn't put in a finishing burst.

But each year they turn up regardless.
They're popular in the parade.
The other teams whistle and cheer them,
aware of the journey they've made.

For the Jungle Olympics in August
They have to set off New Year's Day.
They didn't arrive the year before last.
They set off but went the wrong way.

So long as they try there's a reason.
After all, it 's only a sport.
They'll be back next year to bring up the rear
and that's an encouraging thought.

Richard Digence

31

The Fight

The kick off is
I don't like him;
Nothing about him.
He's fat and soft,
Like a jellybaby he is.
Now he's never done nothing,
Not to me,
He wouldn't dare:
Nothing at all of anything like that.
I just can't stand him,
So I'll fight him
And I'll beat him,
I could beat him any day.

The kick off is it's his knees:
They knock together,
They sock together.
And they're fat,
With veins that run into his socks
Too high.
Like a girl he is,
And his shorts,
Too long,
They look
All wrong,
Like a Mummy's boy.
Then
He simpers and dimples,
Like a big lass he is;
So I'll fight him
Everyone beats him,
I could beat him any day.

For another thing it's his hair,
All smarmed and oily fair,
All silk and parted flat,
His Mum does it like that
With her flat hand and water,

All licked and spittled into place,
With the quiff all down his face.
And his satchel's new
With his name in blue
Chalked on it.
So I chalked on it,
'Trevor is a cissie'
On it.
So he's going to fight me,
But I'll beat him,
I could beat him any day.

There's a crowd behind the sheds
When we come they turn their heads
Shouting and laughing,
Wanting blood and a bashing.
Take off my coat, rush him,
Smash him, bash him

Lash him, crash him
In the head,
In the bread
Basket.
Crack, thwack,
He's hit me back
Shout and scream
'Gerroff me back,
Gerroff, gerroff!
You wait, I'll get you,
I could beat you any day!'

Swing punch, bit his hand.
Blood on teeth, blood on sand.
Buttons tear, shouts and sighs,
Running nose, tears in eyes.
I'll get him yet; smack him yet.
Smash his smile, teacher's pet.
Brow grazed by knuckle
Knees begin to buckle.
'Gerroff me arms you're hurtin' me!'
'Give in?'
'No.'
'Give in?'
'No. Gerroff me arms!'
'Give in?'
'No.'
'Give in?'
'GIVE IN?'
'NEVER.'
'GIVE IN?'
'OOOH GERROOFF GERROFF.'
'GIVE IN?'
'I . . . give . . . in . . . yeah.'

Don't cry, don't cry,
Wipe tears from your eye.
Walk home all alone
In the gutters all alone.
Next time I'll send him flying,
I wasn't really trying;
I could beat him any day.

Gareth Owen

32

Nothing to be Afraid Of

'Robin won't give you any trouble,' said Auntie Lynn. 'He's very quiet.'

Anthea knew how quiet Robin was. At present he was sitting under the table and, until Auntie Lynn mentioned his name, she had forgotten that he was there.

Auntie Lynn put a carrier bag on the armchair.

'There's plenty of clothes, so you won't need to do any washing, and there's a spare pair of pyjamas in case – well, you know. In case...'

'Yes,' said Mum, firmly. 'He'll be all right. I'll ring you tonight and let you know how he's getting along.' She looked at the clock. 'Now, hadn't *you* better be getting along?'

She saw Auntie Lynn to the front door and Anthea heard them saying good-bye to each other. Mum almost told Auntie Lynn to stop worrying and have a good time, which would have been a mistake because Auntie Lynn was going up North to a funeral.

Auntie Lynn was not really an Aunt, but she had once been at school with Anthea's mum, and she was the kind of person who couldn't manage without a handle to her name; so Robin was not Anthea's cousin. Robin was not anything much, except four years old, and he looked a lot younger; probably because nothing ever happened to him. Auntie Lynn kept no pets that might give Robin germs, and never bought him toys that had sharp corners to dent him or wheels that could be swallowed. He wore balaclava helmets and bobble hats in winter to protect his tender ears, and a knitted vest under his shirt in summer in case he overheated himself and caught a chill from his own sweat.

'Perspiration,' said Auntie Lynn.

His face was as pale and flat as a saucer of milk, and his eyes floated in it like drops of cod-liver oil. This was not so surprising as he was full to the back teeth with cod-liver oil; also with extract of malt, concentrated orange juice and calves-foot jelly. When you picked him up you expected him to squelch, like a hot-water bottle full of half-set custard.

Anthea lifted the tablecloth and looked at him.

'Hello, Robin.'

Robin stared at her with his flat eyes and went back to sucking his woolly doggy that had flat eyes also, of sewn-on felt, because glass ones might find their way into Robin's appendix and cause damage. Anthea wondered how long it would be before he noticed that his mother had gone. Probably he wouldn't, any more than he would notice when she came back.

Mum closed the front door and joined Anthea in looking under the table at Robin. Robin's mouth turned down at the corners, and Anthea hoped he would cry so that they could cuddle him. It seemed impolite to cuddle him before he needed it. Anthea was afraid to go any closer.

'What a little troll,' said Mum, sadly, lowering the tablecloth. 'I suppose he'll come out when he's hungry.'

Anthea doubted it.

Robin didn't want any lunch or any tea.

'Do you think he's pining?' said Mum. Anthea did not. Anthea had a nasty suspicion that he was like this all the time. He went to bed without making a fuss and fell asleep before the light was out, as if he were too bored to stay awake. Anthea left her bedroom door open, hoping that he would have a nightmare so that she could go in and comfort him, but Robin slept all night without a squeak, and woke in the morning as flat-faced as before. Wall-eyed Doggy looked more excitable than Robin did.

'If only we had a proper garden,' said Mum, as Robin went under the table again, leaving his breakfast eggs scattered round the plate. 'He might run about.'

Anthea thought that this was unlikely, and in any case they didn't have a proper garden, only a yard at the back and a stony strip in front, without a fence.

'Can I take him to the park?' said Anthea.

Mum looked doubtful. 'Do you think he wants to go?'

'No,' said Anthea, peering under the tablecloth. 'I don't think he wants to do anything, but he can't sit there all day.'

'I bet he can,' said Mum. 'Still, I don't think he should. All right, take him to the park, but keep quiet about it. I don't suppose Lynn thinks you're safe in traffic.'

'He might tell her.'

'Can he talk?'

Robin, still clutching wall-eyed Doggy, plodded beside her all the way to the park, without once trying to jam his head between the library railings or get run over by a bus.

'Hold my hand, Robin,' Anthea said as they left the house, and he clung to her like a lamprey.

The park was not really a park at all; it was a garden. It did not even pretend to be a park and the notice by the gate said KING STREET GARDENS, in case anyone tried to use it as a park. The grass was as green and as flat as the front-room carpet, but the front-room carpet had a path worn across it from the door to the fireplace, and here there were more notices that said KEEP OFF THE GRASS, so that the gritty white paths went obediently round the edge, under the orderly trees that stood in a row like the queue outside a fish shop. There were bushes in each corner and one shelter with a bench in it. Here and there brown holes in the grass, full of raked earth, waited for next year's flowers, but there were no flowers now, and the bench had been taken out of the shelter because the shelter was supposed to be a summer-house, and you couldn't have people using a summer-house in winter.

Robin stood by the gates and gaped, with Doggy depending limply from his mouth where he held it by one ear, between his teeth. Anthea decided that if they met anyone she knew, she would explain that Robin was only two, but very big for his age.

'Do you want to run, Robin?'

Robin shook his head.

'There's nothing to be afraid of. You can go all the way round, if you like, but you mustn't walk on the grass or pick things.'

Robin nodded. It was the kind of place that he understood.

Anthea sighed. 'Well, let's walk round, then.'

They set off. At each corner, where the bushes were, the path diverged. One part went in front of the bushes, one part round the back of them. On the first circuit Robin stumped glumly beside Anthea in front of the bushes. The second time round she felt a very faint tug at her hand. Robin wanted to go his own way.

This called for a celebration. Robin could think. Anthea crouched down on the path until they were at the same level.

'You want to walk round the back of the bushes, Robin?'

'Yiss,' said Robin.

Robin could *talk*.

'All right, but listen.' She lowered her voice to a whisper. 'You must be very careful. That path is called Leopard Walk. Do you know what a leopard is?'

'Yiss.'

'There are two leopards down there. They live in the bushes. One is a good leopard and the other's a bad leopard. The good leopard has black spots. The bad leopard has red spots. If you see the bad leopard you must say, "Die leopard die or I'll kick you in the eye," and run like anything. Do you understand?'

Robin tugged again.

'Oh no,' said Anthea. 'I'm going *this* way. If you want to go down Leopard Walk, you'll have to go on your own. I'll meet you at the other end. Remember, if it's got red spots, run like mad.'

Robin trotted away. The bushes were just high enough to hide him, but Anthea could see the bobble of his hat doddering along. Suddenly the bobble gathered speed and Anthea had to run to reach the end of the bushes first.

'Did you see the bad leopard?'

'No,' said Robin, but he didn't look too sure.

'Why were you running, then?'

'I just wanted to.'

'You've dropped Doggy,' said Anthea. Doggy lay on the path with his legs in the air, halfway down Leopard Walk.

'You get him,' said Robin.

'No, *you* get him,' said Anthea. 'I'll wait here.' Robin moved off, reluctantly. She waited until he had recovered Doggy and then shouted, 'I can see the bad leopard in the bushes!' Robin raced back to safety. 'Did you say, "Die leopard die or I'll kick you in the eye"?' Anthea demanded.

'No,' Robin said, guiltily.

'Then he'll *kill* us,' said Anthea. 'Come on, run. We've got to get to that tree. He can't hurt us once we're under that tree.'

They stopped running under the twisted boughs of a weeping ash. 'This is a python tree,' said Anthea. 'Look, you can see the python wound round the trunk.'

'What's a python?' said Robin, backing off.

'Oh, it's just a great big snake that squeezes people to death,' said Anthea. 'A python could easily eat a leopard. That's why leopards won't walk under this tree, you see, Robin.'

Robin looked up. 'Could it eat us?'

'Yes, but it won't if we walk on our heels.' They walked on their heels to the next corner.

'Are there leopards down there?'

'No, but we must never go down there anyway. That's Poison Alley. All the trees are poisonous. They drip poison. If one bit of poison fell on your head, you'd die.'

'I've got my hat on,' said Robin, touching the bobble to make sure.

'It would burn right through your hat,' Anthea assured him. 'Right into your brains. *Fzzzzzzz.*'

They by-passed Poison Alley and walked on over the man-hole cover that clanked.

'What's that?'

'That's the Fever Pit. If anyone lifts that manhole cover, they

get a terrible disease. There's this terrible disease down there, Robin, and if the lid comes off, the disease will get out and people will die. I should think there's enough disease down there to kill everybody in this town. It's ever so loose, look.'

'Don't lift it! Don't lift it!' Robin screamed, and ran to the shelter for safety.

'Don't go in there,' yelled Anthea. 'That's where the Greasy Witch lives.' Robin bounced out of the shelter as though he were on elastic.

'Where's the Greasy Witch?'

'Oh, you can't see her,' said Anthea, 'but you can tell where she is because she smells so horrible. I think she must be some-where about. Can't you smell her now?'

Robin sniffed the air and clasped Doggy more tightly.

'And she leaves oily marks wherever she goes. Look, you can see them on the wall.'

Robin looked at the wall. Someone had been very busy, if not the Greasy Witch. Anthea was glad on the whole that Robin could not read.

'The smell's getting worse, isn't it, Robin? I think we'd better go down here and then she won't find us.'

'She'll see us.'

'No, she won't. She can't see with her eyes because they're full of grease. She sees with her ears, but I expect they're all waxy. She's a filthy old witch, really.'

They slipped down a secret-looking path that went round the back of the shelter.

'Is the Greasy Witch down here?' said Robin, fearfully.

'I don't know,' said Anthea. 'Let's investigate.' They tiptoed round the side of the shelter. The path was damp and slippery. 'Filthy old witch. She's certainly *been* here,' said Anthea. 'I think she's gone now. I'll just have a look.'

She craned her neck round the corner of the shelter. There was a sort of glade in the bushes, and in the middle was a stand-pipe, with a tap on top. The pipe was lagged with canvas, like a scaly skin.

'Frightful Corner,' said Anthea. Robin put his cautious head round the edge of the shelter.

'What's that?'

Anthea wondered if it could be a dragon, up on the tip of its tail and ready to strike, but on the other side of the bushes was the brick back wall of the King Street Public Conveniences, and at that moment she heard the unmistakable sound of a cistern flushing.

'It's a Lavatory Demon,' she said. 'Quick! We've got to get away before the water stops, or he'll have us.'

They ran all the way to the gates, where they could see the church clock, and it was almost time for lunch.

Auntie Lynn fetched Robin home next morning, and three days later she was back again, striding up the path like a warrior queen going into battle, with Robin dangling from her hand, and Doggy dangling from Robin's hand.

Mum took her into the front room, closing the door. Anthea sat on the stairs and listened. Auntie Lynn was in full throat and furious, so it was easy enough to hear what she had to say.

'I want a word with that young lady,' said Auntie Lynn. 'And I want to know what she's been telling him.' Her voice dropped, and Anthea could hear only certain fateful words: 'Leopards . . . poison trees . . . snakes . . . diseases!'

Mum said something very quietly that Anthea did not hear, and then Auntie Lynn turned up the volume once more.

'Won't go to bed unless I leave the door open . . . wants the light on . . . up and down to him all night . . . won't go to the bathroom on his own. He says the – the –,' she hesitated, 'the *toilet* demons will get him. He nearly broke his neck running downstairs this morning.'

Mum spoke again, but Auntie Lynn cut in like a band-saw.

'Frightened out of his wits! He follows me everywhere.'

The door opened slightly, and Anthea got ready to bolt, but it was Robin who came out, with his thumb in his mouth and circles round his eyes. Under his arm was soggy Doggy, ears chewed to nervous rags.

Robin looked up at Anthea through the bannisters.

'Let's go to the park,' he said.

Jan Mark

Footy Poem

I'm an ordinary feller 6 days of the week
But Saturday turn into a football freak.
I'm a schizofanatic, sad but it's true
One half of me's red, and the other half's blue.

I can't make me mind up which team to support
Whether to lean to starboard or port
I'd be bisexual if I had time for sex
Cos it's Goodison one week and Anfield the next.

But the worst time of all is Derby day
One half of me's at home and the other's away
So I get down there early all ready for battle
With me rainbow scarf and me two-tone rattle.

And I'm shouting for Liverpool – the reds can't lose
'Come on Everton' – 'Gerrin dere Blues'
'Give it ter Number nine' – 'Worra puddin'
'King of der Kop' – All of a sudden – Wop!
'Goal!' – 'Offside!'

And after the match as I walk back alone
It's argue, argue all the way home
Some nights when I'm drunk I've even let fly
And give meself a poke in the eye

But in front of the fire watchin' 'Match of the Day'
Tired but happy, I look at it this way:
Part of me's lost and part of me's won
I've had twice the heartaches – but I've had twice the fun.

Roger McGough

The Seaside

CHORUS
The seaside day begins with empty beaches.
The lapping of the sea and the seagull's screeches;
Slowly the rising sun drives away the cold,
And makes the sea glisten in silver and gold.
Life begins again in a hundred hotels
With sounds from the kitchens and the ringing of bells.
WAITRESS
Here's your tea, sir, here's your tea, sir,
We serve breakfast from eight to nine.
BELLHOP
I've finished polishing your shoes, sir,
And the weather's looking fine.
CHORUS
They sit down to breakfast at the Majestic and the Grand,
The Ambassadors, the Metropole, the Imperial and the Strand.
In Sea View, Chez Nous, and the humblest B. and B.,
And breakfast finished, papers read, they're off to the sea.
WOMAN
Have you got your bucket, Billy, and your spade?
Now don't be silly, Shirley, you be good;
I've got the bathing costumes and the towels.
And Dad has got the basket with the food.
CHORUS
Down to the beach they make their way,
To dig and swim, to sleep and play,
Sprawled in deckchairs and playing cricket,
A few feet of sand and a box for a wicket.
And as the morning burns itself away
From town the crowds by coach and train arrive.
Wearing their comic hats and singing songs,
And happy as the day to be alive.
Oh, we do like to be beside the seaside!
BARKER 1
Any more for the 'Skylark', it's only ten pence a time.
BARKER 2
Candyfloss and ice-cream, and lovely iced-lollies.

BARKER 3

Don't forget your sticks of rock and golden toffee apples.

BARKER 4

Cockles and mussels, and whelks and eels.

CHORUS

This way to the harbour,
   to the pool,
     to the pier,
That's the way to Bingo,
   the dodgems are over here.

SOLO 1

Let's go to the harbour and see the fishing-boats moored.

SOLO 2

Let's go to the swimming-pool and dive off the highest board.

SOLO 3

Let's go to the end of the pier and see the steamer come in.

SOLO 4

Let's have a go at the coconut-shy and see what we can win.

CHORUS

Over here, over there,
   to the pier, to the fair,
Over here, over there,
   follow the crowd with never a care.
Here with a squeal we go round the big wheel.
Round and round and up and down,
And up and down and round and round.

SOLO 5

Oh, I'm so giddy my head's in a spin,

SOLO 6

And I can't hear a word because of the din.

CHORUS

The roundabouts grind out their tinny old tunes,
Military marches
   and songs from the shows,
'Pack up your 'Troubles'
   and 'Anything Goes',
Gilbert and Sullivan, and –
   there's the big dipper
Crawling inch by inch up the steep incline,
Slowly, oh so slowly, oh so very, very slowly,
And then hurtling down like a runaway train.
And now on to the dodgems with a crash, bang, crash,
Clatter clatter clatter, batter batter, bash:
But the day is drawing on now and we're running out of cash,

So let's go down to the sea again for one last splash.
And now back to the station the trippers make their way,
And the stalls and kiosks close again for yet another day,
Like a red ball in the sea the sun is going down,
And the lights are coming on throughout the twilight town.
The seaside day ends with empty beaches,
The lapping of the sea and the seagull's screeches,
The deckchairs have been stacked, the litter cleared away,
And all waits in peace for yet another noisy day.

James Gibson

"Let's dig up father before we go!"

35

Holiday Memory

August Bank Holiday. A tune on an ice-cream cornet. A slap of sea and a tickle of sand. A fanfare of sunshades opening. A wince and whinny of bathers dancing into deceptive water. A tuck of dresses. A rolling of trousers. A compromise of paddlers. A sunburn of girls and a lark of boys. A silent hullabaloo of balloons.

I remember the sea telling lies in a shell held to my ear for a whole harmonious, hollow minute by a small, wet girl in an enormous bathing-suit marked 'Corporation Property'.

I remember sharing the last of my moist buns with a boy and a lion. Tawny and savage, with cruel nails and capacious mouth, the little boy tore and devoured. Wild as seed-cake, ferocious as a hearth-rug, the depressed and verminous lion nibbled like a mouse at his half a bun, and hicupped in the sad dusk of his cage.

I remember a man like an alderman or a bailiff, bowlered and collarless, with a bag of monkey-nuts in his hand, crying 'Ride 'em, cowboy!' time and again as he whirled in his chairoplane giddily above the upturned laughing faces of the town girls bold as brass and the boys with padded shoulders and shoes sharp as knives; and the monkey-nuts flew through the air like salty hail.

Children all day capered or squealed by the glazed or bashing sea, and the steam-organ wheezed its waltzes in the threadbare playground and the waste lot, where the dodgems dodged, behind the pickle factory.

And mothers loudly warned their proud pink daughters or sons to put that jellyfish down; and fathers spread newspapers over their faces; and sand-fleas hopped on the picnic lettuce; and someone had forgotten the salt.

In those always radiant, rainless, lazily rowdy and sky-blue summers departed, I remember August Monday from the rising of the sun over the stained and royal town to the husky hushing of roundabout music and the dowsing of the naphtha jets in the seaside fair: from bubble-and-squeak to the last of the sandy sandwiches.

There was no need, that holiday morning, for the sluggardly boys to be shouted down to breakfast; out of their jumbled beds they tumbled, scrambled into their rumpled clothes; quickly at the bath-room basin they catlicked their hands and faces, but never forgot to run the water loud and long as though they washed like colliers; in front of the cracked looking-glass bordered with cigarette-cards, in their treasure-trove bedrooms, they whisked a gap-tooth comb through their surly hair; and with shining cheeks and noses and tide-marked necks, they took the stairs three at a time.

But for all their scramble and scamper, clamour on the landing, catlick and toothbrush flick, hair-whisk and stair-jump, their sisters were always there before them. Up with the lady lark, they had prinked and frizzed and hot-ironed; and smug in their blossoming dresses, ribboned for the sun, in gym-shoes white as the blanco'd snow, neat and silly with doilies and tomatoes they helped in the higgledy kitchen. They were calm; they were virtuous; they had washed their necks; they did not romp, or fidget; and only the smallest sister put out her tongue at the noisy boys.

And the woman who lived next door came into the kitchen and said that her mother, an ancient uncertain body who wore a hat with cherries, was having 'one of her days' and had insisted, that very holiday morning, in carrying all the way to the tram-stop a photograph album and the cut-glass fruit-bowl from the front room.

This was the morning when father, mending one hole in the thermos-flask, made three; when the sun declared war on the butter, and the butter ran; when dogs, with all the sweet-binned backyards to wag and sniff and bicker in, chased their tails in the jostling kitchen, worried sandshoes, snapped at flies, writhed between legs, scratched among towels, sat smiling on hampers.

And if you could have listened at some of the open doors of some of the houses in the street you might have heard:

'Uncle Owen says he can't find the bottle-opener . . .'

'Has he looked under the hallstand?'

'Willy's cut his finger . . .'

'Got your spade?'

'If somebody doesn't kill that dog . . .'

'Uncle Owen says why should the bottle-opener be under the hallstand?'

'Never again, never again . . .'

'I know I put the pepper somewhere . . .'

'Willy's bleeding . . .'

'Look, there's a bootlace in my bucket . . .'

'Oh come *on*, come on . . .'

'Let's have a look at the bootlace in your bucket . . .'

'If I lay my hands on that dog . . .'

'Uncle Owen's found the bottle-opener . . .'

'Willy's bleeding over the cheese...'

And the trams that hissed like ganders took us all to the beautiful beach.

I remember the smell of sea and seaweed, wet flesh, wet hair, wet bathing-dresses, the warm smell as of a rabbity field after rain, the smell of pop and splashed sunshades and toffee, the stable-and-straw smell of hot, tossed, tumbled, dug, and trodden sand, the swill-and-gaslamp smell of Saturday night, though the sun shone strong, from the bellying beer-tents, the smell of the vinegar on shelled cockles, winkle-smell, shrimp-smell, the dripping-oily backstreet winter-smell of chips in newspapers, the smell of ships from the sun-dazed docks round the corner of the sand-hills, the smell of the known and paddled-in sea moving, full of the drowned and herrings, out and away and beyond and further still towards the antipodes that hung their koala-bears and Maories, kangaroos, and boomerangs, upside down over the backs of the stars.

And the noise of pummelling Punch, and Judy falling, and a clock tolling or telling no time in the tenantless town; now and again a bell from a lost tower or a train on the lines behind us clearing its throat, and always the hopeless, ravenous swearing and pleading of the gulls, donkey-bray and hawker-cry, harmonicas and toy trumpets, shouting and laughing and singing, hooting of tugs and tramps, the clip of the chair-attendant's puncher, the motor-boat coughing in the bay, and the same hymn and washing of the sea that was heard in the Bible.

'If it could only just be like this for ever and ever amen.'

Dusk came down; or grew up out of the sands and the sea; or curled around us from the calling docks and the bloodily smoking sun. The day was done, the sands brushed and ruffled suddenly with a sea-broom of cold wind.

And we gathered together all the spades and buckets and towels, empty hampers and bottles, umbrellas and fish-frails, bats and balls and knitting, and went – oh, listen, Dad! – to the fair in the dusk on the bald seaside field.

Fairs were no good in the day; then they were shoddy and tired; the voices of hoop-la girls were crimped as elocutionists; no cannon-ball could shake the roosting coconuts; the gondolas mechanically repeated their sober lurch; the Wall of Death was safe as a governess cart; the wooden animals were waiting for the night.

But in the night, the hoop-la girls, like operatic crows, croaked at the coming moon; whizz, whirl, and ten for a tanner, the coconuts rained from their sawdust like grouse from the Highland sky; tipsy, the griffin-prowed gondolas weaved on dizzy rails and the Wall of Death was a spinning rim of ruin, and the neighing wooden horses took, to a haunting hunting tune, a thousand Becher's Brooks as easily and breezily as hooved swallows.

Approaching at dusk the fair-field from the beach, we scorched and gritty boys heard above the belabouring of the batherless sea the siren voices of the raucous, horsy barkers.

'Roll up, roll up!'

Dylan Thomas
(Abridged)

The Sea

The waves like ripples,
Crumple
Against withering shores.
The dying foam retreats,
Into the cluster of emerald greens,
Its emotional surface broken,
By quivering breezes,
Showing its freedom,
by violent tantrums that
beat feeble shores.
Then, going back into a tranquil mood,
Almost accepting defeat.

M. J. Josey

Holidays

We didn't manage to have a holiday every year, but when my mother decided that, yes, she thought she could maybe afford one this year, we talked of nothing else for weeks beforehand. We'd sit round the table when my mother came in from work at night and pore over the seaside advertisements in the paper. The ones which drew us like magnets were usually worded, 'Room and kitchen to let, Fair Fortnight,* no linen supplied, attendance if desired, Low door, own key'. The lure lay in the last words. Low door, own key. A low door which opened on to a little side street that ran down to the sea. To us, born and reared in tenements, used to climbing miles of stairs in the course of the year, the excitement of walking right from the street over a threshold which led straight to the living room was a thrill of which we never tired. It was almost like living on the exciting bustling pavement itself, and for my mother and Grannie it seemed like playing at housekeeping.

The minute we got out of the train we would race along the street ahead of Mother and Grannie, searching for the number of our own particular low door. Once, to my joy, our low door was fronted by a *red* doorstep. This was pure fantasy. I didn't know it was achieved by the use of red pipe-clay, and I doubt if I would have believed it if anybody had told me. It was our magic seaside doorstep and I loved it. As soon as the door was opened, we children flew round the house, examining every drawer, every cupboard, the fancy taps on the sink, the fancy handles on the door. Everything was considered 'fancy' which differed from our own at home. While Mother and Grannie laid out our own clean linen and saw to the beds we were sent to the nearest shops to buy something for the tea.

Not for us the doubtful swank of sitting down to somebody else's cooking. We liked to buy and cook our own food. Why, the day might have been blighted from the start if we had been forced to accept what somebody else considered a suitable breakfast, which could be *kippers*, or, worse, *steamed fish*! It was always eggs for us, lovely fresh country eggs, for the country

---

* *Fair Fortnight*: the traditional two week trades holiday in Glasgow.

was no further away than the end of the beach, and we could buy them from the farms any day. My mother had a whole egg, Grannie and I one between us, and the boys one between them, so half a dozen did us for two meals.

It was never any trouble to persuade us to run errands on holiday, for the shops were all so different from those at home.

How absorbing it was to watch the man slice the bacon by hand instead of putting it into a machine. And didn't the milk taste more creamy and satisfying when it came out of a little tap on the side of a huge churn, carried on a cart, pulled by a donkey? Chips from a cart lit by paraffin flares were twice as good as those from a shop, and what triumph to discover for ourselves a bakery which sold the crispest rolls in town, and which served them piping hot, in a bag with scarlet lettering, when we went down to buy them before breakfast each morning.

We worked cheerfully in the fields to help the farmer, regarding the whole thing as adventurous play, and were incredulous when we were given a bag of peas or strawberries as our reward. Our reward for what? For enjoying ourselves? This was paradise indeed. We were allowed by the farmer to go into the fields after the potato-pickers had finished, and keep for ourselves the tiny potatoes which had been left behind as too small to be worth lifting. With these my mother made chips for us, but we had to clean and scrape them ourselves, for she said they were far too fiddling for her. So the three of us would drape ourselves on top of sink and dresser, scraping and scrubbing the marble-sized potatoes, cutting them into minute slices, and at last, blissfully devour plates full of miniature fairy chips.

Seaside ice-cream had a taste all its own too, served between wafers and biscuits intriguingly different from those at home. Some of the ice-cream may not even have been so good as our own Tallies* in Glasgow, but it held fascination for us because it was different. Without ever being told, we knew it was the change which was the best part of our holiday.

The sea was a joy, of course, and distances so impossible to measure in that wide expanse of ocean that I caused great amusement by vowing, the first day we arrived at Girvan, that I was going to paddle out to Ailsa Craig the minute I'd swallowed my tea. I refused to believe it was all of thirteen miles! And it only a wee speck on the map too, and practically joined to the coast.

How golden the sands were, after the earth of our tenement back courts. We made forts, and castles, and leaped from the wall running alongside, and turned somersaults of sheer delight, and after our games, discovered that salt water was far more buoyant than the baths at home, and we could swim satisfying distances without putting our feet down. When we came out, teeth chattering and blue with cold, my mother shuddered and

* *Tallies*: popular name for Italian ice-cream shops.

wondered how we could find pleasure in such icy waters. But to have gone to the seaside and *not* gone into the sea would have been unthinkable, and we pitied the grown-ups who wouldn't take off their clothes and join us in our Spartan splashing.

The pierrots at the end of the sands provided glamorous entertainment. We never went inside the railed-off enclosure, of course, but pressed against the railings and drank in every word and noted every gesture. We loved each member devotedly, but never dreamt of asking for autographs. To us they were beings from another world, and it was unimaginable that we could speak to them. We went to every performance, and knew the repertoire as well as they did, but the moment one of the company came round with the little box for contributions, we vanished. We had no money to give away to people who seemed to us so rich and prosperous, and anyway the 'toffs' sitting inside the enclosure must have contributed *hundreds* of sixpences.

We would have stayed at the seaside all day long, but my mother and Grannie grew tired of sitting there, and we were taken into the countryside on long walks. It seemed all wrong to be walking away from the sea, but soon we were climbing trees, and searching for wild flowers, and hoping Grannie would soon decide she must have a glass of milk and a wee rest. This meant the treat of a visit to a farmhouse, with milk 'straight from the cow' and, on very special occasions, cakes and scones to go with the milk. These treats usually came almost at the end of the holiday, when my mother would look into her purse, count up her money, and decide it was safe to have a little spree. We had already paid for our wee house, so all that was left in the purse was spending money.

And always, on the last day of the holiday, we went to one of the big local houses which had a card on the gate saying, 'Flowers for sale – a shilling a bunch.' We were allowed to stroll round the garden, and Grannie and I made a slow and careful selection of beautiful, scented, old-fashioned cottage flowers to take back with us to our tenement, to remind us of the happy days spent in our own dear wee house, with its low door and its own key.

We always came home on a Saturday morning, to give us plenty of time to get in some food for the week-end, and to give my mother opportunity to get her dungarees ready for her work in the Railway wagon-shop on Monday morning.

Molly Weir

38

Autobiographical Note

Beeston, the place, near Nottingham:
We lived there for three years or so.
Each Saturday at two-o'clock
We queued up for the matinée,
All the kids for streets around
With snotty noses, giant caps,
Cut down coats and heavy boots,
The natural enemies of cops
And schoolteachers. Profane and hoarse
We scrambled, yelled and fought until
The Picture Palace opened up
And we, like Hamelin children, forced
Our bony way into the hall.
That much is easy to recall;
Also the reek of chewing-gum,
Gob-stoppers and liquorice,
But of the flickering myths themselves
Not much remains. The hero was
A milky wide-brimmed hat, a shape
Astride the arched white stallion;
The villain's horse and hat were black.
Disbelief did not exist
And laundered virtue always won
With quicker gun and harder fist,
And all of us applauded it.
Yet I remember moments when
In solitude I'd find myself
Brooding on the sooty man,
The bristling villain, who could move
Imagination in a way
The well-shaved hero never could,
And even warm the nervous heart
With something oddly close to love.

Vernon Scannell

39

The Pleasure Drome

The trouble started at the pleasure drome where the manager didn't want to let me in. He said the pleasure was so strong it could burst my brain. He said I might be able to bear the next show, which was for small kids of seventy and eighty, and he'd think about it. We waited and saw the people from the last show start coming out, and this was when I noticed their feet weren't touching the ground. They came floating out, and they were smiling. They had the weird kind of smiles that angels have in pictures.

We didn't bother asking the manager. We just sneaked in, to the big hall. There were rows of seats circling a central space. There was no stage or screen. There was just a space, with a green carpet. It took a few minutes for everyone to settle. Then the lights went out and some of the kids started whispering, and some of the others told them to shut up.

Nothing happened for a bit, then I realised that in the dark I could see the green carpet, and that it wasn't a carpet but the sea. It was bigger than I thought it was. It was higher than I thought it was. It was all round me and up to my chin, and I could feel it. It was past my chin. I was under it. There was green water all round me.

My heart was thumping, and I heard the kids squealing. I felt Dido hanging on my arm. 'It's okay,' he said in my ear.

We were under water and breathing. I put out my tongue and tasted the sea. I could hear it surging. I could hear it whistling, and singing. It was uncanny singing, without words. It was a low moan going all the way up to a high shriek. It was unearthly and beautiful. It was like no music I'd ever heard; fascinating, of another world.

'Whales,' Dido whispered in my ear. 'The whales are singing.'

And suddenly, in a colossal great smother of foam, three of them sprang up; massive whales, at least eighty feet long. They flashed past me, and I saw the whole length of them, mouths to tails, and swung round in my seat, and saw them fanning off in the sea all around. All the sea was lashed into luminous foam, and I heard the kids squealing, and saw their arms flickering up under water like seaweed to try and touch the whales.

There was a fantastic volume of sound as the whales tore

around and sang, and spiralled upwards, and we went up with them; up and up through glorious green depths, with the water suddenly sparkling and lightening, until we burst right out of it, and the whales blew.

They blew huge spouts of water. We were cascading in the air with their spouts, and then had left them behind.

They were far behind, far below.

I could see them below; three whales, flicking their fan tails on the surface of the sea: tiny whales now, because we were going fast. We were going at fantastic speed. We were rushing through the air, and all the kids were squealing again because all around the blue sky was whistling with our speed, and we were in the world above.

My brain was spinning. The world was spinning. I could see it below me, and our rocket dizzyingly turned, so that the world lurched upwards, until it was level, and I could see its curve. I saw the curve of the earth. I saw tiny mountains standing up, like on a relief globe. The globe slowly span. I saw Spain, and France. I saw Britain. I saw the finger of Cornwall. I saw where Polziel must be!

I saw ocean, and Canada and the eastern coast of America all the way down to Florida; the whole shape of it slowly turning, until the distance was too great, and no detail could be seen, just the whole globe turning, turning. And also turning blue.

The globe was blue now: a beautiful little planet, enclosed in its atmosphere, receding fast, at hundreds of thousands of miles an hour.

It was whistling darkness now as the planet contracted; into a tiny sapphire, into a bit of diamond dust, into nothing.

The kids had stopped squealing. In the rushing darkness, there was a kind of awe, and the rocket slowly revolved once more, and a little bright star passed on our left, with a tiny scatter of dust about it, and Dido said in my ear, 'The sun. The solar system.' And it was gone.

All gone. Everything was gone. There was nothing anywhere. There was no light. There was a roaring darkness, that was thudding, and thudding rhythmically. It was thudding like a heart. It was my heart. All of me was thudding, my feet, my hands, my hair. I was part of the thudding. I was suddenly a part of everything, of the whole universe, of space. I was smaller than my own pulse. I was a beat in everything's pulse. I didn't exist. I hadn't been born. It was all blackness.

It was fantastic blackness.

I'd never known such blackness. I couldn't see any of myself. I couldn't even feel myself. I couldn't believe the blackness. In the darkest room, on the darkest night, behind closed eyes, you couldn't see such blackness. If you stared hard enough you could always see something, a fleck.

I stared as hard as I could. I stared so hard my eyes ached, but I got a fleck. I got a spark. It was like a pain. It was red so I knew it was blood from the veins behind my eyes. Then it grew bigger, and I knew it wasn't.

The spark was there. It hung in the blackness. It was brighter than a cigarette end, redder than a ruby. It was bigger than an egg, than a balloon, than the moon. It wasn't even red. In the thudding vibrations, it was changing colour. It was rose, and pink, apricot, peach, pearl. In steady throbbing waves it expanded everywhere.

It washed over the front rows, and I heard the gasps of delight and saw the kids standing up; and felt it coming towards me, and got the first tremor myself. The sound was changing, too. The light was washing the harshness out of it. It was melting and softening into music. Then it touched me and a single gasp came out of me. I felt I was just born, out of nothing. I felt I was a baby being bathed. I felt I was being picked up. And unbelievably I was. The kids in front weren't standing. The light had lifted them. We were all floating in it.

Now there were all colours, blue, silver, amber, emerald, and they were rippling through me. The colours and the sounds were going through me. I seemed to be shimmering in long ripples of pleasure. They got so intense, they came so fast, I could hardly bear it. Just when I couldn't bear it, and heard myself gasping again, a clear tide of sapphire blue washed through me.

Everywhere the kids were gently floating. Dido was floating beside me. We were all smiling the weird smiles; we couldn't help it. I don't know how long it went on. There were several more of the spasms. They got stronger. The feeling of happiness was almost painful. Then it became softer and gentler, till we were lowered to our seats again, and there was a smell of flowers everywhere. I could smell them as we went bobbing out into the night. I couldn't feel the ground. It was like treading water. I was just full of pleasure.

I was so full of it I forgot to tell him again not to do anything dangerous with me.

And my time had come now. It was here.

Lionel Davidson

Pantomime Poem

'HE'S BEHIND YER!'
chorused the children
but the warning came too late.

The monster leaped forward
and fastening its teeth into his neck,
tore off the head.

The body fell to the floor
'MORE' cried the children

'MORE, MORE, MORE

MORE

MO

Roger McGough

Daddy-Long-Legs

In the last rays of the sun
A daddy-long-legs flew
And though his life was nearly done
He felt as good as new.

But to him it seemed a shame
That he'd soon disappear
Without one single claim to fame
To show that he'd been here.

And so he drifted on the breeze
And he'd not gone too far
When he was sucked into the ventilator
Of a cinema.

And there upon the silver screen
A dancing man appeared

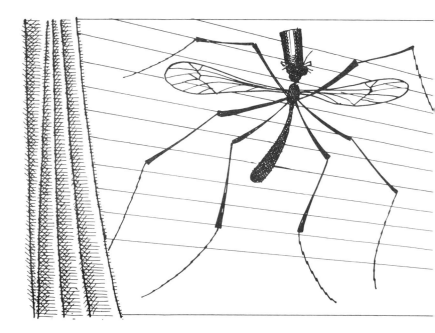

In top hat, white tie, tails and cane
And everybody cheered.

Then up into the beam of light
The daddy-long-legs flew
And on the silver screen
His shadow started dancing too.

Daddy-long-legs, dancing to the beat.
Daddy-long-legs, two people, eight feet.

As the man in tails tapped out each step,
Daddy-long-legs danced as well
Until somebody swatted him
And to the ground he fell.

And as he lay there fading fast
He said, 'What do I care?
I'm the only daddy-long-legs
To have danced with Fred Astaire.'

Daddy-long-legs, dancing to the beat.
Daddy-long-legs, two people, eight feet.

Jeremy Lloyd

42

What Makes Us Laugh?

I like the **Lenny Henry** show. He imitates people like doctors, break dancers etc. But he emphasises the characters and what they do. That's what makes me laugh.

Donna

Nothing gets me to laugh so much as funny comedy programmes and stupid jokes and silly rhymes.

Cheryl

Dianne

I like 'Spitting Image'. President Reagan would be on his motor bike with Nancy and he would have his nose pierced and wearing leather jacket and trousers.

My favourite TV comedy show is 'The Young Ones' because it is disgusting and vulgar. Apart from that it's quite good.

Samantha

Comedies usually have someone acting really stupid which makes other people laugh. If someone hurts themself by tripping over a chair for example, you sometimes laugh then have to put on a serious expression. I find it funny if someone is eating something really disgusting like what Fungus the Bogeyman eats which are mouldy cornflakes, bogies, flies and mouldy anything. I think that if someone is doing something and gets it wrong, you can laugh at that too.

Siobhan

I like Benny Hill because he's rude.

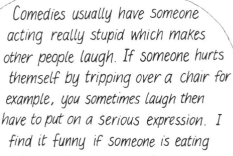

Danny

The Form Master

The boys are seated at their desks. JOHN *starts to call the roll.*

JOHN: Aggeridge, Ankerton, Borby, Bungabine ... (*As he says each name a boy says 'here'*) Cloistermouth, Cuthbun, Hogg, Lipstrob, Mudd, Muffet, Munn Ma., Orris, Root...

CUTHBUN: Please, sir,

JOHN: Yes ... er ...

OMNES: Cuthbun, sir.

JOHN: Yes, Cuthbun?

CUTHBUN: Mr Pelham used to make a joke there sir; he used to call them out together, Orris root you know sir.

CLOISTERMOUTH: They use it for scenting soap.

ORRIS: And we used to answer together, Root and me, sir.

CUTHBUN: Root and I.

BUNGABINE: And we all laughed ... haw haw haw!

JOHN: All right ... er ...

OMNES: Bungabine, sir.

JOHN: Bungabine. That will do. Terhew, Trindle, Unman, Wittering and Zigo.

OMNES: Absent!

JOHN: Yes, so I understand.

CLOISTERMOUTH: He was ill, sir.

UNMAN: With an unknown disease, sir.

LIPSTROB: And his father took him to Jamaica, sir.

CUTHBUN: To recover, sir.

ORRIS: And when he has, he'll come back, sir.

AGGERIDGE: That's why his name's still on the list, sir.

JOHN: Yes, thank you.

CUTHBUN: Jamaica's in the Caribbean, sir.

JOHN: Yes, Cuthbun, I know that.

TERHEW: Have you ever been there, sir?

JOHN: No.

AGGERIDGE: Mr Pelham went there once.

TERHEW: Twice.

AGGERIDGE: Once, the other time was Trinidad.

CUTHBUN: He went to Jamaica the time he went to Trinidad as well.

JOHN: Quiet! (*There is complete silence*) This is all very interesting, but not to the point. (WITTERING *screams with pain*) Who was that? (WITTERING *moans*) You? What's your name?

WITTERING: Wittering, sir.

CLOISTERMOUTH: Wet Wittering, sir.

JOHN: Quiet. Come out here, Wittering.

(WITTERING *comes out and stands in front of* JOHN'S *desk*)

CLOISTERMOUTH: Mr Pelham called him Wet Wittering, sir.

JOHN: Quiet! Now, Wittering, why did you make that noise?

WITTERING: Sir, I was jabbed, sir.

JOHN: Jabbed?

WITTERING: With a compass, sir.

JOHN: Who jabbed you?

WITTERING: I don't know, sir.

JOHN: Well, go back to your place and wipe the ink off your chin.

WITTERING: Sir.

JOHN: And I don't want any more fooling about, or there'll be trouble.

CUTHBUN: Sir?

JOHN: Cuthbun?

CUTHBUN: I don't understand, sir.

JOHN: What do you not understand, Cuthbun?

CUTHBUN: 'I don't want any more fooling about or there'll be trouble.' It doesn't make sense, sir. Do you mean there'll be trouble if you do want fooling about?

JOHN: I mean that if there is any more fooling about, verbal or practical, there will be trouble.

CUTHBUN: Oh, I see, sir, yes, sir.

CLOISTERMOUTH: Mr Pelham always told us we had to be frightfully careful with our English, sir.

JOHN: And he was quite right, Cloistermouth. Now then: McMorrow and Purdie's history of England, chapter nine. *(The class noisily get out their books and open them)* All right, all right. *(Silence)* Has anyone read chapter nine?

TERHEW: Yes, sir.

JOHN: Good . . . er, Terhew. Perhaps you'd give us an outline of its contents.

TERHEW: Me, sir, oh no, sir.

JOHN: And why not?

TERHEW: I haven't read it, sir.

JOHN: You said you had.

TERHEW: No, sir, you asked if anyone had read it and I said yes, sir, Cuthbun has.

BUNGABINE: He's read the lot, sir.

TRINDLE: The whole book.

CUTHBUN: It ends with the General Strike.

JOHN: Does it? Well, tell us about chapter nine.

CUTHBUN: Actually, sir, I left that chapter out. Terhew was wrong.

TERHEW: I'm most terribly sorry, sir.

JOHN: Shut up, Terhew.

TERHEW: But I am, sir, really.

JOHN: Why did you leave that chapter out, Cuthbun?

CUTHBUN: Because Mr Pelham said the Wars of the Roses were not worth bothering about.

CLOISTERMOUTH: Yes, he did, sir, really.

JOHN: Oh, in that case we will read it together.

CLOISTERMOUTH: But, sir.

JOHN: Yes, Cloistermouth?

CLOISTERMOUTH: Mr Pelham did say, sir.

CUTHBUN: And if it's not worth bothering about surely it's a waste of time reading it.

JOHN: I consider that they are worth bothering about.

UNMAN: Mr Pelham was quite definite, sir.

JOHN: Nevertheless we will read it.

AGGERIDGE: Sir, please, sir . . .

JOHN: Yes, Aggeridge?

AGGERIDGE: May we have a window open?

JOHN: No.

AGGERIDGE: Mr Pelham said it was bad for our lungs to work in a stuffy atmosphere.

CUTHBUN: And Aggeridge has to have good lungs, sir, he's in the second eleven.

JOHN: Well I think it's bad for us to work in a draught. Begin reading, Wittering.

WITTERING: Me, sir?

JOHN: Yes, go on.

WITTERING *(Slowly):* 'The Wars of the Roses. In fourteen fifty-three at the colse . . .

JOHN: What?

WITTERING: Colse.

JOHN: Spell it.

WITTERING: C-L-O-S-E.

JOHN: Which is what?

WITTERING: Close. *(He pronounces it with a soft 's')*

JOHN: No, close.

WITTERING: '. . . close of the Hundred Years War, England was in a . . .

JOHN: Well?

WITTERING *(Rushing at it):* Condescension . . .

JOHN: No, Wittering! A *condition* bordering upon anarchy. Can't you read?

TERHEW: Not aloud, sir.

JOHN: I asked Wittering.

CUTHBUN: Mr Pelham never put him on to read. He said life was too short.

JOHN: I asked Wittering.

BUNGABINE: Mr Pelham's life was too short. Haw haw haw.

JOHN: Quiet! *(Silence)* Now I don't wish to crack the whip on our first morning together, but I will if you make me. I want no further interruptions.

CLOISTERMOUTH: But, sir . . .

JOHN: Did you hear me?

CLOISTERMOUTH: Sir, Mr Pelham said we were always to ask if we didn't know anything.

JOHN: I do not care what Mr Pelham said.

OMNES: Ooh, Sir!

JOHN: Now look here. I know his death must have been a great shock to you, but life goes on and there is work to be done. We will get through this chapter this morning, or if not we will do it this afternoon.

TERHEW: But sir, it's a half-holiday.

JOHN: Yes Terhew.

AGGERIDGE: And there's a second eleven match.

JOHN: Yes, Aggeridge. Continue reading.

AGGERIDGE: 'Many of the nobles were virtually little kings, raising their own armies and levying their own taxes.'

(During this, UNMAN *begins muttering)*

UNMAN: Hypotenuse, hypotenuse, hypotenuse . . .

AGGERIDGE: 'The authority of the Crown . . .'

JOHN: Stop. Who is muttering?

UNMAN: Me, sir.

JOHN: Unman, did you hear what I said?

UNMAN: Yes, sir.

CLOISTERMOUTH: He can't help it, sir.

CUTHBUN: He says hypotenuse, sir, all the time.

TERHEW: He likes the word.

AGGERIDGE: Mr Pelham said he was hypotenused by it.

(General laughter)

JOHN: Stop! *(Silence)* Very well. You have had your warning. The form will stay in this afternoon from half-past two until I am satisfied with your behaviour.

(Pause)

CLOISTERMOUTH: It's not a good idea, sir.

JOHN: No Cloistermouth? Tell me why not.

CLOISTERMOUTH: Well, sir, Mr Pelham did it once.

CUTHBUN: The week before last, sir.

CLOISTERMOUTH: And that was why we killed him.

(Dead silence as JOHN *hastily writes on a piece of paper)*

JOHN: Cloistermouth, take this note to the headmaster.

CLOISTERMOUTH: Now, sir?

JOHN: At once.

CLOISTERMOUTH: What does it say, sir?

JOHN: That you have been insolent.

CLOISTERMOUTH: But, sir, I haven't. Only truthful.

OMNES: That's right, sir.

JOHN: Go on, Cloistermouth.

CLOISTERMOUTH: No, sir.

JOHN: Very well. Then I shall fetch the headmaster here.

CLOISTERMOUTH: You'll look an awful fool, sir.

JOHN *(Shouting)*: Get out!

CLOISTERMOUTH: If you hit me, sir, there'll be a terrific row.

TERHEW: Form masters aren't allowed to hit us.

CUTHBUN: You'll be sacked.

AGGERIDGE: And after all, he was telling the truth, sir.

CLOISTERMOUTH: I always do.

JOHN: Oh yes? and how did you kill Mr Pelham?

LIPSTROB: We murdered him.

CLOISTERMOUTH: On Signal Cliff, sir.

CUTHBUN: That's the big one on this side of the town.

CLOISTERMOUTH: He always went there for a walk in the afternoon, sir. The day after he'd kept us in we waited for him.

TERHEW: Six of us.

CUTHBUN: In the bushes.

CLOISTERMOUTH: He came up quite slowly, panting a bit.

TERHEW: And he paused at the top and took out his handkerchief.

CUTHBUN: The fog was coming in from the sea.

CLOISTERMOUTH: Then we came out from the bushes all round him. He started to say something...

LIPSTROB: But we rushed him and got him on the ground.

AGGERIDGE: Rugger tackle.

CLOISTERMOUTH: His specs fell off and he started lashing out.

BUNGABINE: So we hit him on the head with a stone.

ORRIS: K.O.

LIPSTROB: Gedoing.

TERHEW: Then we carried him to the edge and chucked him over.

BUNGABINE: A'one, a'two, a'three ... and away!

CLOISTERMOUTH: And there was blood on the stone, so we threw that over too.

ORRIS: Dead easy.

CUTHBUN: Nobody saw us because of the fog.

BUNGABINE: The perfect crime. Haw haw haw.

JOHN: Hardly.

CUTHBUN: Why not, sir?

JOHN: If you had done it . . .

OMNES: We did.

JOHN: You would have spoilt it all by telling me. Your vanity would have given you away.

CLOISTERMOUTH: But we have told you, sir.

JOHN: And if I believed you I'd tell the police . . . through the headmaster of course.

CUTHBUN: But that wouldn't do any good, sir. You don't know which of us did it.

JOHN: The police would find out. They'd get you one by one and question you.

TERHEW: We've all got alibis, sir.

CLOISTERMOUTH: Yes, sir, really we have. I was in Chapel with Unman and Muffet, polishing the candlesticks.

CUTHBUN: Terhew, Hogg and me were having tea in Orris's study.

LIPSTROB: Aggeridge, Root and Trindle were playing fives with me.

BUNGABINE: I was in the armoury with Borby and Ankerton. We were cleaning our equipment web for the C.C.F. parade.

WITTERING: And Mudd and Munn and me were doing detention.

CUTHBUN: I mean to say, sir, we can prove it. There are at least two witnesses for every member of the form.

(The HEADMASTER *enters)*

JOHN: Oh, Headmaster.

HEAD: Carry on, Mr Ebony. Take no notice of me.

JOHN: Er . . . yes . . . er

CUTHBUN: The battle of St Albans, 1455, the battle of Wakefield, 1461.

JOHN: Fourteen sixty, Cuthbun.

CUTHBUN: Sorry, sir, Hedgely Moor and Hexham, 1464. *(The* HEADMASTER *goes out)* He's gone. There you are, sir, we're good at alibis.

Giles Cooper